A PLACE IN SCOTLAND

MANAGING DIRECTOR Sarah Lavelle

EDITORIAL DIRECTOR Sophie Allen

SENIOR DESIGNER Gemma Hayden

PHOTOGRAPHER Alexander Baxter

PERMISSIONS MANAGER Samantha Rolfe-Hoang

PRODUCTION DIRECTOR Stephen Lang

SENIOR PRODUCTION CONTROLLER Sabeena Atchia

Quadrille, Penguin Random House UK, One Embassy Gardens, 8 Viaduct Gardens, London SW11 7BW

Quadrille Publishing Limited is part of the Penguin Random House group of companies whose addresses can be found at global.penguinrandomhouse.com

Penguin
Random House
UK

Published by Quadrille in 2024

www.penguin.co.uk

A CIP catalogue record for this book is available from the British Library

ISBN 978 1 83783 199 9
10 9 8 7 6 5 4

Colour reproduction by F1

Printed in China by C&C Offset Printing Co., Ltd.

The authorised representative in the EEA is Penguin Random House Ireland, Morrison Chambers, 32 Nassau Street, Dublin D02 YH68.

Penguin Random House is committed to a sustainable future for our business, our readers and our planet. This book is made from Forest Stewardship Council® certified paper.

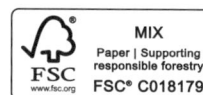

MIX
Paper | Supporting responsible forestry
FSC® C018179

A PLACE IN SCOTLAND

BEAUTIFUL SCOTTISH INTERIORS

———

BANJO BEALE

Photography by ALEXANDER BAXTER

quadrille

Contents

Introduction

———

Something is happening in Scotland. A new confidence – and inspiring new voices – are redefining what 'Scottish style' really is.

From merchant houses reimagined for the 21st century to windswept castles rescued from ruin, Scotland is home to some of the most remarkable homeowners, architects, designers and craftspeople lacing our spaces and places with a new verve.

Stone bothies nestled in the Highlands and blackhouses on the edge of islands are at once preserving history and adding new chapters with modern additions. Victorian coaching inns have become beacons for international art and tiny tenement flats are reinventing how we live, work and play in our city neighbourhoods.

As we embark on our grand tour through Scottish design you are warmly welcomed inside these remarkable spaces. Although wildly different in budget and style, they are united in a shared history, inspired by nature and our neighbours and packed full of wit and whimsy.

HISTORY

The people and places making their mark today have not forgotten the past. Instead, they are embracing history to peel back years of neglect (and tartan wallpaper) to return spaces to their former glory. There will always be room in our collective hearts for tartan and tweed, but traditional emblems are being reimagined and repurposed, with new dream weavers adding their spin, mixing contemporary art, heritage crafts and international influences to create a new, rejuvenated vernacular.

NATURE

From royals to watercolourists to royal watercolourists such as Queen Victoria, it is the wide open spaces, wild glens, glassy lochs, majestic Munros and long sandy beaches of Scotland that have long been beacons of natural beauty. Today, our spaces not only seek to make the most of our surroundings, but also to create the least impact possible. New homes are lightly bedded into the landscape and traditional dwellings are updated with restraint, creating quiet spaces to sit still and embrace the rhythms of nature.

Our materials and palettes are transforming hotels and homes into moody meccas inspired by the rugged beauty on our doorstep, with stone and wood, earthen lime plaster and natural textures. Meanwhile, bright young things are animating their homes with the colours of the wildflowers and machair of our Hebridean islands.

NEIGHBOURS

Our Norse neighbours have long been a part of Scottish history and today their influence is apparent in our Scandi Scot aesthetic, combining minimal interiors with design classics. For every hygge home in Copenhagen there is a nook to 'coorie' into in Scotland – coorie being the Scots word meaning snuggling and nestling into a space. Our warm nests are antidotes to long, dark winters. The trade winds even blow all the way to Japan and in exchange for our whisky we have imported wabi-sabi, celebrating the imperfection and impermanence of our homes.

HUMOUR

The Scots keep their tongues firmly planted in their cheeks at all times. In fact, the phrase itself first appeared in 1828 in the novel *The Fair Maid of Perth* by Sir Walter Scott. A sense of playfulness extends to our spaces, with refined hotels outlandishly adorned in flying stags and ancient castles bedecked in bearded ladies.

BRAVERY

From turning a World War II control tower into a family home to raising children in a castle ruin, it takes a brave, hardy and sometimes foolhardy person to rehabilitate and create spaces in wild and woolly places. For those souls who saw potential to add new energy to abandoned buildings, their bold endeavours are rewarded with a place in history, like castle custodians carving their new family motto in stone above their door: challenge accepted wisdom.

From the verdant forests of the Cairngorms to the brooding seas of the north, we hope you find somewhere in this book to admire and inspire with imaginative, humble, grand and outlandish places to stay, play and stray.

These dwellings are the set pieces to some remarkable lives. When we are welcomed inside, we come to learn that it is people who make places. You're invited to go behind the scenery to meet the rebels, raconteurs and entrepreneurs who are bravely writing a new chapter in Scottish design.

Rodel House

ISLE OF HARRIS, OUTER HEBRIDES

———

Historical Reimagining

Rodel House is 'at the end of everything', noted poet Louis MacNeice upon visiting this handsome Hebridean outpost in 1938. Standing proudly on the southern tip of the Isle of Harris, with views out across the Isle of Skye, this is a building with quite a tale to tell.

The lunar landscape here is dotted with hard Harris rock, only broken up by lochs and long, curving, white sandy beaches. This is crofters' country, where hardy Hebrideans make a living from farming and fishing and where ornithologists, archaeologists, botanists, surfers and intrepid explorers make pilgrimages.

Built in 1781 by Captain Alexander Macleod, Rodel was made, like most island dwellings, from what you could get at the time. Lairds – owners of large estates – have come and gone here, their plans to regenerate the island and turn it into a money-making proposition dashed against the wild weather and rock.

In its heyday, Rodel has been a hotel, storehouse, fishing lodge and a pub with a clock that famously ticked backwards, much to the chagrin of crofters' wives. Rodel has long been the scene of salty yarns and a respite for queens, rebels and ratbags.

Those who muse on the splendour of years gone by recall the royal yacht *Britannia* anchoring here in the 1950s – and how, outside Buckingham Palace and the late Queen's personal homes, this unlikely spot was the only place in Britain you could procure a rare dram of Royal Household Whisky.

In 2001, this gentle giant rose from the ashes following a full renovation by local crofter Donnie MacDonald, whose family had owned the hotel since the 1930s.

Deterioration led to the closure of the house in the 1970s – except for the public bar. Gradually, rooms and entire wings became dilapidated and redundant and were closed off. The salt-saturated gales whipping up the Sound of Harris ripped the slates and the felt from the roof, prised the sarking from the rafters and marinated the interiors.
R.M. Murray, Isle of Lewis writer

A patchwork of reclaimed materials sourced from the British Isles invoke the feeling of a ship's cabin, while vintage and contemporary designer pieces sit side by side.

The hotel was restored, rebuilt and reborn yet again by Francine Stone and Anderson Bakewell, one of the founders of the Isle of Harris Distillery and owner of the nearby uninhabited island of Scarp. Harris has been his spiritual home since he first visited in the 1960s. A musicologist, Bakewell has orchestrated the latest remodel, composing a medley of experts and craftspeople to reimagine the space as it may originally have been intended to look.

Lachlan Stewart of ANTA interiors took the house back to its Georgian footprint, taking time to understand the building's origin, stripping it back before building it up again. With the precision of boat builders, local tradespeople added a softwood frame that now sits inside the exterior. The exterior is lime-washed, using an old Georgian recipe to protect it from the whipping salt winds; its pointing contains crushed seashells.

Old and new sit seamlessly together here, with reclaimed materials including an old gymnasium floor from Dundee and teak for the bathrooms – all arriving on site as puzzle pieces to put together. Retrouvius, London-based interior designers and reclamation experts, led the sourcing for the interior fit-out, prioritising texture, patina and a healthy dose of restraint, allowing the building to once again sing against the flinty waves, glinting sun and salty air.

The attention to detail, craftsmanship and consideration that has gone into every fixture, finish and piece of furniture is deftly apparent and not until you stay in the space can you fully appreciate its deliberate design, right down to the teak-topped bathtub that has been shaped to perfectly nuzzle Mr Bakewell's head. The handmade Zellige tiles, with Delft tile accents, complete the most relaxing bathroom experience.

Left: Limewash paint bounces the soft Hebridean light around cosy and vast spaces alike.
Right: a drawing room with attached whisky snug and library make for a perfect respite from the wild weather outside.

A homely hearth and timber panelling frame the view out onto the pier and islands beyond.

The cost of living in the Outer Hebrides is long, dark winters. Sunrise and sunset dance gloriously across the lime-washed walls here, as if the sun knows it's here for a good time, not a long time. When the light has almost faded into the gloaming, the rich panelling of the drawing room takes centre stage, the peaty fire is lit and the whisky drams are poured.

When the weather is 'dreich' (Scottish for dull and dismal), the best feature in the grounds comes into its own: the sitooterie, a combination of sitting and oot, a Scot's way of staying out. Here, a sitooterie has been built into the walled garden and becomes the perfect perch from where to watch the wild weather roll by.

Harris is perhaps most famous for its tweed, celebrated at Rodel in a contemporary twist, with one dashing room treated to an upholstered wall and ceiling. The cosy, cocooning effect of the tweed is the ultimate expression of coorie.
Each of the bedrooms in Rodel has been

drenched in one strong palette and material, enveloping the space and inviting its guest to hurkle durkle – a long-forgotten 19th-century turn of phrase that means to stay in bed long after it's time to get up.

Materials and crafts from the past have been embraced at Rodel to create what feels contemporary and historic at once. Everything here has been done with reverence to its wild and sacred location and, more importantly, built to last the next 230 years.

Zellige tiles with Delft accents surround the reclaimed timber-clad bath. An iroko top has been moulded to nestle the soaker's head.

Q&A with Christopher Nisbet, house manager

___

Favourite elements you brought to the space?

The care and attention to the correct historical detail. For instance, every window has its own bespoke wooden shutters, the lime render is made to a traditional recipe, the lime pointing contains crushed seashells and the Georgian fireplace works like a dream.

How did the collaboration work between owner, architect and designer?

The best evidence of the owners' collaboration with Lachie Stewart of ANTA interiors, the architect, and Maria Speake of Retrouvius, the interior designer, are the noises of appreciation of any guest as they cross the threshold and explore the house for the first time – and maybe nostalgic surprise as they discover the dumb waiter.

Design muse?

The 18th-century adventurer and builder of the house, Captain Alexander Macleod.

Favourite place to sit and enjoy what you've created?

The window seat by the fireplace in the first-floor drawing room, which looks out over the piers, the Rodel Estate's three islands – Balaigh, Flodaigh and Corr Eilean – and then 22 miles across the Minch to Dunvegan Castle on Skye.

What music is playing?

Lena, our local 14-year-old player of the bagpipes. We like to encourage local talent.

Dream Scottish house guest?

It has to be Captain Alexander Macleod with his tales of sailing the Indian Ocean in the 18th century, where he made his fortune, and his return to Harris.

House drink?

A generous dram of our recently released single malt whisky The Hearach, preferably taken in front of a peat fire.

Somewhere close to play?

A quiet moment spent in the nearby 16th-century church of St Clements and the graveyard around it, which tells the history of this wild and ancient place and the people who sought to make it their home. A wander along the golden sands of Scarista beach with its distant view of St Kilda. For fit folk, the panorama of the Outer Hebridean Isles offered from the summit of our village's mountain, Roineabhal.

Somewhere in Scotland to stray?

The architecture of Edinburgh always makes a dramatic backdrop to whatever one has to do there and a complete contrast to a life now spent on Harris, where we have no traffic lights and only one roundabout – which is mostly ignored.

HMS Owl

FEARN, THE HIGHLANDS

———

Air Control Tower

HMS Owl is a four-storey brutalist brick tower built in 1942 on Fearn Airfield in Tain in the Highlands. During World War II, Fearn Airfield was one of Britain's most important naval airfields, with the Barracuda Operational Training Unit and the No. 2 Torpedo School both sited there. The tower was closed in 1957, falling into disrepair, finally being transformed over five years into a family home by Justin Hooper and Charlotte Seddon.

This was an unusual restoration project. Transforming its crumbling shell was a messy job after years of occupation by only the livestock that sheltered here during winter. Only after excavating a foot of cow dung could work begin.

The first port of call was deciding on windows. Forty per cent of the budget was then spent on adding Crittall windows. At airfields all over the country, huts fitted with Crittall standard windows used to house Spitfire and Hurricane pilots during the lulls between their battles.

Seven hundred panes of glass and an army of ironmongers were needed to create the windows that would have once lit the space. It was important for business owners Charlotte and Justin to add the real McCoy here and pay homage to British manufacturing history (and a time when women were window fitters). As the demand for manpower grew during the war, women took over an increasing share of the work in factories. Metal windows were still required for camps, barracks, emergency hospitals, government factories, hostels and airfields – including HMS Owl.

The next big decision was what to insulate and cover up and what to leave exposed. Finding the balance between what to do with their remaining money, keeping its industrial feel, and making it a warm space was the biggest challenge of all. The more time Justin and Charlotte spent with the building the more they fell in love with its rugged industrial feel. Crumbling concrete pillars were preserved, ceilings and floors and contrasting exposed brickwork all add to the industrial modernist interiors.

My seat at the kitchen table is my favourite spot. I love so many of the different views and quiet corners in the house, but I most love sitting at our annoying and beautiful wobbly, splintery kitchen table and talking to the children or my guests. I can also see who's coming and going – like you should be able to do at all good control towers.

Warm timber and the familiar homely comforts of charity-shop finds harmoniously contrast the raw and exposed concrete walls and painted black pylons.

Warmer touches come in the form of leather and wooden furniture and a wood-burning stove, which takes pride of place in the living room. In fact, the house is dotted with large horizontal fires and ample wood piled high. Warmth is always nearby should you need it. Big rugs and plenty of cushions are flung about in what Charlotte describes as a 'scatterbomb approach', adding to its well-lived-in feel.

The amazing lateral house has taken a long time to fill and Charlotte says she doesn't think she will ever move, just keep adding to it. This is a home that doesn't take itself too seriously, as kids and animals rule the roost. The children, Agnes and Bert, and their mates, love it as a popular get-together house. 'That's what I love about it, it's tough and cool as a house and can absorb a lot of people on its many levels.'

The control tower is all about the views out to the airfields, torpedo sheds and farmland beyond.

In its relatively short life this home has lived and has many tales to tell. 'When the planes are flying from the runway and all the animals and people are fed, it feels bloody brilliant to live at HMS Owl.'

A vintage bath, exposed brick and an old junk shop cabinet-come-curiosity case create a timeless and calm space.

The main living space works hard and plays hard. The foosball table sits alongside a jungle of plants and a black Togo sofa.

Q&A with Charlotte Seddon

Favourite spot to enjoy what you've created?

My seat at the kitchen table. I love so many of the different views and quiet corners in the house but I most love sitting at our annoyingly beautiful, wobbly, splintery kitchen table and talking to Agnes and Bert and whoever is here. I can also see who's coming and going like you should be able to do at all good control towers.

Design muse?

Part of what worked in creating this place was my partner and I had different tastes and our roots in very different budgets – his was 1980's advertising, and mine was being a florist.

Dream Scottish house guest?

Lewis Capaldi or Billy Connolly.

Who is spinning on the record player?

The Young Ones rule the record player here at HMS Owl. More likely Gardeners Question Time on my watch. And Granny Charl – I can't pretend to be cool.

House drink?

A good flat white or a pint of pale rosé.

Somewhere close to play?

ANTA for some really great brownies and homewares, which is around the corner from Owl. Torguish House at Daviot for a root through their old Nissen huts for stag's heads, garden antiques and a million other interesting bits. Dingwall Mart rare breed sale to watch or buy some interesting looking sheep, goats, hens and cows. We're about to put a big, reclaimed, black corrugated barn up and hopefully fill it with more animals... and stuff.

Somewhere in Scotland to stray?

Shandwick beach – swimming, and a coffee flask at the ready, then back to the house for a hot tub.

Wormistoune

CRAIL, FIFE

———

Legends & Lore

Wormistoune is the home of the mythical Scottish Wyrm, a fearsome dragon-like serpent allegedly slain by a medieval knight on the mound. Today the Wyrm, in the form of a cast creature, hides in plain sight, patiently watching over the McCallums, the new Baron and Lady of this 17th-century tower house and garden.

Sitting on the edge of the East Neuk, close to the royal burgh of Crail in the Kingdom of Fife, this deliciously warm ochre, lime-washed home has played host to ancient family feuds, artists and, as legend has it, it was the last place in Scotland where witches were tried.

A sign over an external door of the castle reads, 'challenge accepted wisdom'. Its new caretakers have taken this invitation and boldly run with it. Both house and garden have been painstakingly restored over the past 20 years and while it remains intertwined with Scotland's own rich history of serpents, sorcery and ancient adventurers, its new owners have bravely made their mark.

The castle spans clans, from Balfour to Lindsay to Spens, whose most famous son was Admiral Sir Patrick Spens of the ancient Scots ballad of the same name. One of the oldest ballads in Western Europe, it tells the story of a king who seeks an experienced sailor in his kingdom for a dangerous journey.

Swapping building sandcastles with their children to restoring a real castle with a sometimes dark history was not a journey for the faint of heart. It was the call of Spens that brought the McCallums on what, at times, felt like an impossible mission to preserve the storied building. A sense of history, playfulness and a profound respect for the past has helped them craft a series of spaces that will no doubt secure their own mark on history.

It took more than 18 years to complete the castle – much like raising a child – and, of course, there were growing pains. Buying the castle as a series of walls, they restored the house to what it was, adding another floor and a half to meet it where it was once taller.

The king sits in Dunfermlin town,
Drinking the blude-red wine;
'O where will I get a skeely skipper,
To sail this new ship o' mine?'

The Ballad of Sir Patrick Spens

A hand-painted wooden ceiling adorns the dining hall with vignettes of Wormistoune's past and present, from the poetry of Robert Burns to the adventures of Sir Patrick Spens.

At once grand and snug, this timeless sitting room, wrapped in a warm limewash and topped with timber beams, helps to make this castle a home.

The castle and its gardens are like a worm themselves, revealing the history that winds through its heavy oak doors and around its grounds. It reaches its pinnacle in the grand hall where the ceiling is a masterpiece of hand-painted wood, depicting bygone scenes from the estate, bringing the home and its history of loyalty and loss to life.

Up the spiral staircase, the house reveals its Georgian side. The elegant, lovingly restored drawing room overlooks the garden's Celtic love knot parterre and over to the 15th-century 'doocut' or dovecote.

Overlooking the vibrant garden rooms of the historical walled garden that adjoins Wormistoune, a coach house with rich interiors echoes the heritage of the main house, enhanced with more contemporary touches. At every turn, the secret garden rooms of Wormistoune embrace a totally new character. Enter through the knot parterre, a hark back to Enlightenment Scotland, where puzzles and riddles were the ultimate sophisticated flex.

From the order of the maze, enter the wild, vibrant pathway to the ancient orchard, following the Wyrm's tail into the garden's 'great hall' – a visceral and delicate space where the colours change almost weekly as new flowers bloom and life explodes. Continue along the Wyrm's tail, and enter the dark and mysterious cavern of Wormistoune's enchanted forest. Suddenly, the openness and colour gives way to soft hues of green and textures of bark and stone. Hidden somewhere along the old stone wall, flanked by ancient trees, the Wyrm reveals itself with dramatic flair.

Antique furniture, timber and candlelight create artful vignettes in every corner.

*Earthy, pigmented plaster
walls connect the spaces
whilst the cooling grey
contrasts with the warm
linen to make a fresh
attic respite.*

Q&A with Gemma and James McCallum

What was your design approach?

Each building has a relationship to its location as well as the influence of those who built it and have lived and worked in it. I believe that you need to live in a space for a while, untouched, for it to 'speak' to you before you can truly understand what it needs. Age, architectural style and location are of course a huge factor, but once you get to know the bones and soul of a building, you can begin to add your, and your family's, own style. Lots of designers have a signature style that they successfully replicate in different places for different clients, but I believe each space is individual – making it your own allows you to become part of its unique history.

Design muse?

There are so many extremely talented designers that I admire. They create truly beautiful spaces and I am in awe of many of them and their work. As an 'amateur' architectural designer and interior stylist, my main inspiration is my mum. My mum was an art school student when I was very young, studying fashion. Her eye for the smallest of details, along with adding unexpected elements, have influenced my style and given me confidence to not worry about mistakes, as even they can be a wonderful surprise. My mum created wonderful family homes and she was always ahead of her time.

Favourite spot to enjoy what you've created?

At our kitchen table, sitting with James and our children (young adults now), eating dinner and debating the world and its issues. Our children have their father's very dry humour and they can make each other laugh like no others can. It's the best sound in the world. For James, it is sitting on the wooden bench beside the Lochan at sunrise, looking back at the house and listening to the morning birdsong.

Who is spinning on the record player?

Crail local, King Creosote (Kenny Anderson), album *From Scotland with Love*.

Dream Scottish dinner party guest?

Beatrice M.L. Huntington. Born in St. Andrews, she travelled around Europe at a time when it was almost unheard of for a women to travel on her own. She studied painting, sculpture and music, laterally becoming known for her portraiture work. She moved to Edinburgh and established a 'salon', inviting musicians, artists and writers for dinner and conversation. She was known for her love of poetry, music and enthusiasm for life; a perfect dinner guest! She died aged 99 in her sleep, after hosting a late-night party!

Somewhere close to play?

All of the fishing villages along the coastline are a must: St Monans, Elie, Pittenweem, Anstruther and, of course, Crail. Cambo Gardens, Kingsbarns Distillery, Bowhouse for its monthly markets, Futtle for the best locally made beer and music, Crail Harbour Gallery and Tearoom, Kilconquhar Inn for world class food, the list can go on and on...

Somewhere in Scotland to stray?

Kingsbarns beach any day, any time of year, but our family favourite is heading down to Crail Harbour on a sunny day with a bottle of wine and grabbing some freshly cooked crab from The Crab Shack or a takeaway from Crail Harbour Gallery and Tearoom and sitting on the wall of the harbour watching the boats and people coming and going.

Bluebell House

BEARSDEN, EAST DUNBARTONSHIRE

———

Pattern on Pattern

This Arts and Crafts house was built in 1912 in Bearsden, on the fringes of Glasgow, towards the end of an era defined by simplicity in design, natural elements and a belief in objects being well made, useful and decorative. Its owner, Fi Douglas, continues the tradition over a century later, adding her own signature floral flair, while highlighting the home's original features with bold colours.

Fi's family hails from the Outer Hebrides, where wildflowers carpet the 'machair'. This Gaelic word refers to the grassy land along a sandy shore, and one of Scotland's most remarkable living landscapes. The machair is one of the rarest habitats in Europe, where a mix of sand, made up of crushed shells blown ashore by wild Atlantic gales, and crofting practices have formed a rich mosaic of grassland teeming with wildflowers and bustling with bird and insect life.

Like the machair, where people manage the land in a way that encourages wildlife, Fi has managed to etch a family home and a livelihood from wildflowers, with her design practice Bluebellgray. Business is blooming for Fi and her home is a canvas on which to experiment with colour and print.

Scottish bluebells are also called harebells as it's believed the witches used to turn into hares and hide among the flowers. While there is nothing wicked about this home, Fiona has cast her magical spell across its walls, adorning them with her favourite flowers, which appear all around the property in spring.

The dark days of a Scottish winter can feel long and, although they are beautiful in their own way, Fi misses colour. She started her business with the primary focus of bringing joy into people's lives through colour and subsequently, her family home.

For Fi it is just as much about wellbeing as it is joy. 'I really believe your environment affects how you feel, and it's an often overlooked part of our wellbeing. Looking at something that you personally find beautiful or uplifting every day is a great and relatively simple way to elevate your mood and day.'

Living in Scotland I've always felt very affected by the weather and my environment. Growing up surrounded by beautiful views brought me a lot of happiness, peace and a deep appreciation for nature that I truly didn't comprehend the effect of until I was an adult.

A wildflower wall, designed by the homeowner springs to life behind a pillowy linen sofa with a menagerie of patterns and colour.

Dark panelling has been refreshed with spearmint paint and a mix of vintage and contemporary art and objects add a playful touch to this family home.

The home is painted in shades of blue and green throughout, the colours of the bluebells and the beaches blanketed by the machair grass and flowers, proving once and for all that the adage 'blue and green should never be seen' is simply not true. Accents of orange and pink miraculously create a calm, technicolour scheme.

Fi feels a duty of care to decorate her home in a way that honours the house and its surroundings, seeking to add colour and the mood-enhancing effects of light. Taking advantage of the house's incredible natural light, Fi has sought to enhance it as much as she can. Making this home feel like her own and creating a warm, welcoming, fun family home with no rules for her family has been her number one priority.

Colourful and joy filled, this home celebrates history, provenance, the handcrafted and of course pattern and colour – all cornerstones of the designer's work – helping to create an authentic and charming space. There's a confident mix of bolder 'hero' motifs with softer ginghams and stripes, vintage furniture (sometimes painted in bold colours), an element of natural wood mixed with an anchoring paint colour.

Of course I wanted to add my own stamp to this house, but with a house like this, which has so much history and character, I didn't want to do anything that would take away from its charm; and in anything I did, decorating-wise, I wanted to retain original features and make those features sing, while still making it feel like our home.

The big and little kids in this home have received the designer treatment, with a keleidoscope of fabric, from the floor to the ceiling.

Q&A with Fi Douglas

What was your design approach?

As a designer, I wanted to embrace the original features while adding my own special touch to make it feel like home. The wallpaper and murals I have designed were inspired by our garden and it's a way of adding my own bit of history and honouring the Arts and Crafts heritage of the home, a movement so inspired by nature and flowers.

Favourite elements you brought to the space?

Colour, softness and warmth. Despite the huge windows, the house had a very dark feel when we moved in; lots of very dark varnished wood overwhelmed the space for me and made it feel quite formal and cold. I love the coloured window frames, the sanded-back original floors and the bespoke wallpapers I added – they make the house feel light and joyful.

Design muse?

My favourite ever interior is the White House (No.39 Arnol), owned by Historic Environment Scotland in the village of Arnol on the Isle of Lewis. My family roots are from the next village and the interiors are the most honest and beautifully real I've ever seen. I always feel a sense of familiarity when I visit. I love the use of colour, and nothing is contrived, which makes it so special. It reminds me of the houses of my grandparents and old aunties we visited when we were kids. I also love the vintage pieces; it's very much part of my signature style to use colour, vintage furniture and pattern. I adore Scotland with all my heart, but I find the dark nights and long winters hard sometimes. Bringing colour to my interiors is important for my creative mind and brings lightness to those long rainy nights in deep winter.

Favourite spot to enjoy what you've created?

The bay window in my studio on a sunny day. It looks out to the garden and sitting there with the sun streaming in is pure interiors joy.

Who is spinning on the record player?

I love Scottish music, Tidelines and Skipinnish are two bands from where I grew up that are always on repeat in our house.

House drink?

Harris Gin, always.

Dream Scottish house guest?

My kids and I love the Scottish comedian Susan Calman. She would be our dream Scottish house guest.

Somewhere close to play?

We have a little cabin on the west coast. It's got a sea view and escaping there, switching off and watching the sunset, while my kids play and run around in freedom, is my absolute favourite thing in the world to do. It's a pretty magical spot, full of nature, and I've had a lot of fun making the cabin a special place for my family.

Somewhere in Scotland to stray?

I'm a Highland girl so the west coast has a special place in my heart. I love all the Scottish islands but Gigha is a hidden gem, it's tiny and perfectly beautiful and has the most amazing seafood. The Boathouse is my favourite place for seafood in Scotland. You eat right on the edge of a sandy beach and the view is stunning. The Nook takeaway is a favourite too – you can sit on the beach enjoying fish and chips, bliss.

Lundies House

TONGUE, SUTHERLAND

———

Wild & Refined

This far-flung 19th-century stone manse overlooks the Kyle of Tongue, a silvery sea loch at the top of Scotland. North of the majestic Ben Loyal, a Munro known as the queen of Scottish mountains for its distinct peak, Tongue is a crofting township along the north coast. The area was a crossroads for the Gaels, Picts and Vikings who once inhabited the area and are responsible for its unusual name – Tunga is Old Norse for a piece of land shaped like a spit or tongue.

The town's most infamous moment comes courtesy of Bonnie Prince Charlie. In 1746 it was the scene of a sea chase, a shipwreck and a skirmish when the ship *Hazzard*, carrying £13,000 (two million dollars today) in gold to fund the Jacobite Rebellion, was forced to run ashore at Tongue. The Jacobite crew unloaded the chests of gold with the intention of carrying it away overland, but tossed it into the loch when government troops caught up with them. Some of the gold was recovered, but the search still continues!

Today, the area is a pitstop on North Coast 500, a grand tour of Scotland and the country's answer to America's Route 66, where the Highlands' rugged beauty is exhibited in all its glory. Driving beside the North Sea to majestic beaches, the route takes you through sweeping glens and past fairytale castles and ruins right to the front door of Lundies.

Behind the scenery, Wildland, an organisation dedicated to rehabilitating natural landscapes, have become custodians of Lundies House and a vast swathe of land that has been planted with over six million trees. Efforts to reduce deer numbers are helping to reverse the impact of overgrazing and restore balance here, while the conservation continues in Wildland's historical buildings, which have been carefully restored.

Inspired by a deep sense of place, this Victorian clergy house has been transformed by its Nordic owner into a 'wee hotel' and combines refined interiors and a profound sense of comfort to create somewhere of simple beauty and stillness – a base camp which reflects the raw and unspoilt landscape that surrounds it. Lundies House is a beautiful marriage of unique Scottish vernacular and contemporary Scandinavian design.

Original details have been preserved by Wildland alongside Edinburgh-based architects GRAS, with flagstone floors, plastered ceilings and shuttered windows anchoring the house in timeless tradition. The addition of Scandinavian design pieces, influenced by the owner's homeland, bring a modern take on the building's heritage. Work from eminent Danish artists sits alongside bespoke furniture and cabinetry from Scottish makers.

The property is surrounded by Highland hills, silver birch, lavender and slopes awash with heather, all of which are reflected here in the restful finishes and fabrics. The bedrooms, all painted in a natural, soothing colour palette, add to the sensation of being huddled from the temperature shifts of Scotland's rocky Highland coastline. A muted gorse colour wraps its mustard weave around the living room alongside warm velvets and tactile bouclé fabrics.

Timber cladding envelops the eaves to create a space to coorie away from the north coast weather.

The top-floor bedrooms and living spaces have been seamlessly slotted underneath the eaves and add to the feeling of being sheltered in a moss-lined cave. The bath, in fact, looks out to the ruin of Castle Varrich, the ancient seat of the Clan Mackay. (It is believed that clan members once inhabited caves under the castle, although the caves remain undiscovered, and the ancient castle may in fact be built on an old Norse fort.)

In the dining room, an atmospheric wall mural by French botanical artist Claire Basler depicts grasses and wildflowers set against a moody grey sky, bringing the wild outside in. Oak, marble, washed linen and a natural material palette add to the serenity throughout Lundies.

Outside, reclaimed slate and brick and Crittall windows sit effortlessly within the dry stone walls, with native woodland planting and ground cover allowed to naturalise. Hard surfaces such as concrete have no place here, and growth is encouraged to spill over on gravel paths to ensure nature is never entirely kept at bay.

This artful reimagining of a house into a boutique hotel feels at one with its historical context and future sustainability. The only chaos here comes from the howling wind and the swallows hurling in and out of eaves. Then again, there is something quite relaxing about that, too.

Left: a wildflower wall mural in a warm and moody palette enlivens the senses in the dining room. Right: calming neutrals and warm textiles anchor the communal spaces and bedrooms.

CHRISTIAN LEMMERZ

Cosy bouclé wingback
chairs provide inspiring
places to commune.

Q&A with Nathan Tucker, house custodian

What was your design approach?

The design and concept are all down to Ruth Kramer, I look after the maintenance and upkeep of this unique space, I am merely the custodian.

Design muse?

The beach: the contrast between sand, stones, and the dunes, the mix of textures, colours and sounds created from the waves and ocean – nature at its most powerful and creative.

Favourite spot to enjoy what you've created?

My back garden, my private escape. The views overlook the mouth of the Kyle of Tongue, the rabbit islands and beyond to Orkney. From here the summer night sky shows off sunset, moonrise and Venus, all lined up in a row to form a celestial showcase.

What music is playing?

Music is my eclectic pleasure, anything from classical to electric, and I have always had a passion for the sounds of Hôtel Costes.

Dream Scottish house guest?

An evening dinner is a rarity for me owing to the demands of my time and the business; if I ever get the opportunity, it is always with family or my partner.

House drink?

Gin is my go-to, I am in love with Lind & Lime, distilled in Edinburgh, it has a distinct hint of pink peppercorn, perfect mixed with a citrus.

Somewhere close to play?

I am a homely soul when it comes to play, the opportunity is so scarce owing to the demands of work, any downtime for me is with my partner, around the firepit in the evening summer sun, or next to the log burner of a cold winter evening.

Somewhere in Scotland to stray?

It's always the beach, I have my own 'secret beach' I visit near my home. I feel most at home, next to or in the ocean.

Gifford

EAST LOTHIAN

———

Modern Love Story

Katie and Jordan Laird met in an Edinburgh bar designed by modernist architect Ian Arnott. Years later they would buy a house in East Lothian and go on to realise it was designed by the same architect. It wasn't exactly love at first sight for one of the creative couple. Jordan, a director, was not entirely smitten with the house. Katie dragged him to a viewing to be nosy and, although they adored it, he took some convincing to leave the city. However, not wanting this to be the one that got away, they put in an offer on Friday and had it accepted on Monday.

It was a big move for this family of five, who have only lived at Gifford for two years. Some people escape to the countryside for extra room, but as it turns out their Edinburgh flat had more square footage. Hidden doors, a sprawling garden and an open-plan concept make it a place the family have come to thrive in. Arnott got it right back then. However, when it was built in the 1960s it was so progressive that neighbours complained about it to the local press. If they dared change it today, there would be equal outrage.

The house comprises a series of boxes, as Arnott described them, arranged around a central living space, as well as angled pop-ups in the roof – made from the same slate as the roof of the nearby church. Katie and Jordan also bought a lot of the Arnott's modernist furniture and still have the same curtains. They have added new touches, including a chequerboard tile floor in the kitchen, mid-century modern furniture and some new pieces, albeit things that look as if they have been made for the house, such as a bench from the furniture school up the road.

When it comes to decorating Katie, a fashion stylist, looks to her mum as her muse. 'My mum's style is built-in. That's who I learned about style from. She's a classic – cashmere, straight leg jeans, blazers, loafers, trench coats. I've stolen her clothes since I was about nine years old.' This building is being dressed the same way, celebrating the classic staples and bringing in modern pieces to avoid it looking like a time warp. Katie likes to accessorise with bold text-based graphics, experimenting with colours from her other muse, a young David Hockney. Vintage pieces, classics and works from maker mates sit side by side in this creative home. Nothing here is too precious, it feels as if it's casually thrown together, as only a supremely stylish couple could do.

Katie and Jordan also like to play detective, figuring out why things were done the way they were in the first place. The architect sadly died in 2022 and he is buried across the road, a forever reminder for Katie and Jordan not to mess the building up. The family now has a house they can expand into and while respecting the original vision, there is a lot they plan to do that Arnott might approve of. In fact, it might even be his original idea. There were lots of drawings left behind that he had drafted for this place but, like many people, hadn't got around to doing. Katie and Jordan plan on making the carport into a bedroom and connecting it to the house. And seven-year-old Sonny has big plans that there will also be a swimming pool in the garden one day.

A curved vintage sofa and piles of magazines create a cool and contemporary feel.

Plants and playful art allow the home's mid-century features to sing.

Left: a checkerboard floor
is a modern, retro update.
Right: original joinery
adorned with modern
sculptural pottery respect
the building's past.

A typographic tapestry is an invitation to this creative family to stay weird.

Q&A with Katie Laird

What was your approach to designing the space?

Restore as much as possible but modernise it with sensitivity to its character and the era.

Favourite elements you brought to the space?

Colour: I think this house would look stunning in neutrals, but we couldn't help but inject a bit of colour with the artworks. The tiled floor: we tried hard to embrace neutral colours, but the pattern made them more fun. Family: this was built as a family home, and we brought the chaos.

As a couple, how did the collaboration work?

We are both creative people so we worked together, we collaborated and inspired each other. This gave us the confidence to change things up.

Design muse?

The architect who designed the house, and who recently passed, is definitely the design muse. Every time we change something, it's a version of what he originally created, but with our spin on it. And we only do things we hope he'd approve of. He's buried across the road, and I imagine he's keeping an eye on it.

Favourite spot to enjoy what you've created?

Sitting in front of the window, looking out into the garden. One window looks out into lots of trees. You can imagine living in a forest if you squint your eyes.

Who is spinning on the record player?

Young Fathers, Frightened Rabbit and Vampire Weekend.

House drink?

Margarita of course!

Dream Scottish house guest?

Billy Connolly.

Somewhere close to play?

The Free Company – beautiful food in a beautiful setting. It doesn't get much better.

Somewhere in Scotland to stray?

East Neuk of Fife, a place we gather with our close friends, eat well and drink too much…

Allt-A-Bhruais

SPEAN BRIDGE, LOCHABER

———

Self Preservation

Anja and Jan Jacob left the Netherlands over 20 years ago and have settled into a new life in this characterful, treasure-filled home in the Scottish Highlands. The whitewashed cottage is not as humble as it first appears, nor as old. Built in 1937, this home is a curious contradiction with grand fireplaces, built-in bookcases and a staircase that looks as if it belongs in a castle. Delusions of grandeur, or just an architect who sought to create a modest home in a baronial style?

The rustic charm of Anja and Jacob's home is inspired by its location and the owners' vocation as venison charcuterie producers – with antlers featuring prominently throughout the space. 'As we work with deer-based products, these are a true reflection of our area and where we live. They have their own space though – too much and it becomes a trophy room.'

When Anja and Jan Jacob start designing or doing up a room, the first stop is a rummage in one of their sheds to work with what they have, always favouring salvage yards, charity shops and skips over buying new. The parquet floors were crafted from leftover lengths of timber and the kitchen was made from doors and drawers that came from a school in Aberdeenshire. These thrifty owners collect things, from homeware to hardware, whenever they see something or fall in love with the material, often without an immediate purpose for them. When it came to designing the kitchen, the number of drawers was dictated by how many they had found, and the same with the cabinet doors. Here it is a case of adapt and fit, and fit and adapt again.

The kitchen is where the family spends most time, with its original Norwegian slate and wood-fired cooker a central feature of this cosy space. The tiles are new, but made just like they were hundreds of years ago. Called 'witjes', they are reminiscent of those you see on Dutch Old Masters. Anja and Jan have had them in every kitchen they have built over the years.

When adding new pieces to their home, the owners are looking for pieces that have a story to tell. Perhaps their surface shows that they have been used and loved for many years, adding soul to the space through their worn patina. It could be a milking stool that is smoothed from years of use or a vintage rug that shows the passing of time through a distressed finish. They all hold stories, and add so much to the atmosphere of each room.

Design choices revealed themselves at Allt-a-Bhruais as decorating began. When stripping the house to its original core, turquoise wallpaper appeared that would go on to inform paint choices, while wreaths and flowers adorn the space from whatever grows nearby. At the heart of all designs and layouts there is a practical blueprint that favours functionality and beauty. Like the owners' produce, here are simple ingredients, crafted with care.

Colourful glassware and candle holders provide the perfect vessel to display the garden's bounty.

Left: the spiral staircase would not look out of place in a castle.
Right: TBCo x Banjo Beale tartan blanket and sheepskin throws add warmth and texture at the handsome family dining table.

Old-school cabinets painted teal complete with the bumps and bruises of a kitchen well-worn.

Q&A with Anja Baak

Favourite spot to enjoy what you've created?

The kitchen, where everything happens –
the woodfired Esse is always on and everyone
gathers around the kitchen table.

Dream Scottish house guest?

Our six children, it is so special when they
come home, especially when it's all of
them here together.

What music is playing?

We usually have BBC Radio 3 or classic FM in
the background, but love a good Scottish trad
band too – local bands Tidelines and Breabach
are our favourites.

What are you serving?

A platter of our wild venison charcuterie with
Scottish cheeses, figs and grapes.

Somewhere close to play?

Camasdarrach beach, between Mallaig
and Arisaig on the stunning west coast, is
somewhere we love to drive to for the evening.
We take a picnic and watch the sunset.

Somewhere in Scotland to stray?

Dunkeld is our favourite place to stay. We
always stop on our way down south along the
A9. A refuel at Arran bakery is a must for a
delicious pastry, and an overnight stay at the
Taybank, perfectly positioned by the rushing
river is an absolute treat.

Bard

THE SHORE, LEITH

———

Crafted

The historic port of Leith on the north shore of Edinburgh has served as a gateway for goods for centuries and was once Scotland's main trading port. It's from here that two debonair modern merchants are introducing Scottish craft and design to a new audience.

Bard feels more like a collector's home than a shop. Named for the Celtic word for storyteller, its curated edit of objects weaves a story of artists and makers, past, present and emerging. Shopkeepers Hugo Macdonald and James Stevens have transferred the salt-of-the-earth hospitality they receive in the kitchens, studios and workshops of craftspeople into the experience at Bard, ensuring the space feels like the home of your most eccentric and cultured friend.

There are no shortages of places to sit, whether it's wooden 'creepies' (stools used for milking cows) or an early 20th century Arts and Crafts revival chip-carved chair, based on the crofter's chair from Caithness. Or perhaps it's Scotland's most celebrated example of vernacular furniture, the Orkney chair, typically made of driftwood and straw and designed to keep the draughts at bay.

Hugo, a design writer and curator who grew up on the Isle of Skye, and James, an architect and interior designer, have created a layered space that feels deeply rich and textured. Downstairs, burnt sienna plaster walls drench the rooms, while an imposing table draped in thick vintage linen acts as a canvas for earthen tableware and totems.

Upstairs, pine floors have been left raw while the whole space has been plastered in raw earth pigments to bring out a natural tactility. This space is an architectural and craft experiment in pigments, tone and luminosity.

Rustic woven willow baskets from the Isle of Eigg contrast with soft Fair Isle throws and a traditional Victorian five-seater sofa.

The overarching ambition for this divine depository is to be playful, with clashes of colour, material and texture, and not overly curated. As Hugo and James say, 'There are, or should be, no rules when it comes to living with the things you love.'

We imagined a young creative who inherited an old-fashioned property from his grandparents and is bringing his more punk aesthetic into the mix.

Fishing rope has been recast into a majestic hanging sculpture by artist Mark Cook and a ceramic and metal leaf lozenge by James Rigler quietly rests on the landing.

Left: an Orkney chair rests on a jute rug while a Shetland Woollen Co. jumper floats on the pigmented plaster wall. Right: burnt sienna walls create the perfect backdrop for modern artefacts.

The feeling here is of a Georgian New Town living room, with punctuations of Orkney and Shetland. The story is that it's a young couple who split their time between their refined Edinburgh home and a back-to-nature bothy up on Orkney.

Stone and wood are suspended in mid air in Oliver Spendley's sculptures while a handsome sofa takes this space from gallery to home.

Q&A

with Hugo Macdonald and James Stevens

What was your approach to designing the space?

JAMES: We wanted to create the feeling of home. Bard is about inspiring people to live with craft and design. So much craft today gets treated either like a museum artefact or an untouchable artwork. We like demystifying it – taking objects off plinths, not hiding them behind glass. There are no Do Not Touch signs. Designing a feeling of home felt like the surest way to help people feel comfortable, relax, ask questions and – importantly – imagine how they might live with these objects themselves in their own homes. Bard is like a serving suggestion in that sense. Our early discussions around a story for the building were always to imagine it as the home of a collector – someone with a voracious appetite and eye for exquisite objects, materials and stories, found and made, old and new. Half the people who come in ask if we live here, which feels gratifyingly like we succeeded in our aim!

HUGO: James has a special knack for designing feelings and atmospheres rather than relying on Pinterest boards of reference images. I love the storytelling aspect of his design process because I can join in. I have an overactive imagination and can embellish the characters and scenarios wildly. James brings them to life. Our ambition to create the home of a collector was poetic and practical. It gave me licence to bring my own hoarding of ephemera – books, stones, weird objects – into the mix among the craft and design. On a more practical note, it allows us to rotate, rejig, refresh and edit constantly. The layering is rich and intense, and the frequent changes bring fresh energy – and reasons for people to visit us more than once!

Favourite elements you brought to the space?

JAMES: We have more questions about our earth-pigmented plaster wall finishes than almost anything else. They are warm, tactile and feel inherently 'made'. As such they're the perfect backdrop and a welcoming canvas against which to show a range of different materials of different ages.

I designed the freestanding shelving system as Bard's first piece of furniture design. It is a modular system using Douglas fir and ash ladders that are held in tension between the ceiling and floor. The ash insert shelves can be moved around as desired. Verticality is so important in all rooms, and especially the soaring ceilings found in Edinburgh's New Town. The ghost rope (discarded fishing rope, pulled up by fishermen) knotted hanging by Mark Cook from Orkney, suspended in the stairwell, is a powerful piece in its own right. It was also a conscious decision to suspend something in this lofty space to animate it and turn the stairwell into an event. We want to encourage people to be courageous with filling space, not just walls and surfaces! The shadows it casts on the plaster when the sunlight bounces off the water of the Leith outside, are extraordinary.

HUGO: On our first weekend open in chilly November, we realised we could never have the doors open all day, so James installed an old fashion pull bell, and we put a sign out to ask people to pull it. What started life as a heating hack has been one of our most successful tricks. People love ringing the bell, so we open the door to smiling faces (almost) every time. And we get to greet and welcome everybody into Bard, which helps set the tone – again like a home. People tend to behave differently with more open curiosity and respect, rather than browsing and ignoring us then leaving.

As a couple, how did the collaboration work?

JAMES: It's an ongoing process – like love and life generally! I tend to treat Hugo like something between a muse and a client. He's too opinionated to involve in every decision, we'd never get anything done. So we talk about broader concepts and imagine scenarios and feelings we want to create and inhabit together. He's a good critic and he has a great wealth of references from his background as an editor.

HUGO: It's very different working with your partner. We've both worked for couples a lot in our careers to date, all of whom warned us, and have been generous mentors! Letting each other be good at the things we're naturally good at is harder than it might sound. I thought I'd be good with people but I get terrible stage fright, and take everything very personally! I'm much happier behind the scenes. For our studio projects we do concept development together, then James lets me lead on strategy. He takes over with the design work and we share creative direction. I look after communication.

Design muse?

JAMES: We embellished our imaginary collector whose home we are constantly designing with Bard. There are elements of Hugo and myself in there. Hugo has eccentric tastes and a hoarder mentality. Sometimes this alights on strokes of genius; other times, I follow closely behind, tweaking.

HUGO: Bard is an open exploration of Scottishness, and there are lots of Scots whose approaches to life (rather than design or interiors) have fed into our imaginary collector: Mary Queen of Scots, The Immortals, Nan Shepherd, Sharleen Spiteri, Flora Macdonald, Clare Grogan, Margaret Fay Shaw, Kelly Macdonald, the knitters of Fair Isle, Penny Martin and Tilda Swinton of course. Intrepid,

melancholic, powerful. Dancers to the thrum of their own drums, all.

Favourite spot to enjoy what you've created?

JAMES: I am mostly to be found upstairs. Upstairs is intentionally soothing – somewhere to pause and sit and take things in. It is lighter, luminally and spatially. Like the dream drawing room of a Georgian flat in the New Town. We reupholstered a large, upright six-seater Victorian baronial sofa in a rough porridge wool from the Isle Mill. With the help of some sheepskins Dougal has made it his home-from-home.

HUGO: I like being downstairs. It's darker with a burnt umber pigment and some larger pieces of brown furniture. James imagined it with the feeling of a weighty inheritance – as if someone had inherited a dour baronial pile and was beginning to inhabit it with their own art and object collection. It feels riotous and mournful simultaneously. We've got giant hogweed in there at the moment, as if our incumbent protagonist is losing their mind slightly, wrestling to make peace with their dastardly ancestor who left them a castle with a leaking roof.

Who is spinning on the record player?

JAMES: Never Enya! Cruising craft to a soundtrack of wailing Celtic voices is too much.

HUGO: We do enjoy our 80s and 90s pop, and the incongruity that comes with discussing earnest matters of craft with guests while Britney sings about pole dancing. Discord is every bit as important as harmony.

Dream Scottish house guest?

JAMES: I always say that having Bard feels a bit like an endless house party – you just never know who's coming. Mercifully, we haven't yet had to throw anyone out!

HUGO: Any of our Scottish muses – preferably all at once. Can you imagine the noise and fun?

Somewhere close to play?

JAMES: Leith is filled with excellent places. We describe it as Copenhagen with edges. A perfect day begins with coffee and outrageously filled almond croissants from Williams & Johnston. We'll walk these off with Dougal along the Water of Leith to Edinburgh Sculpture Workshop. This is followed by a lengthy lunch at The Shore Bar – a Scottish–French bistro with curved banquettes that hold you like a hug, and the most incredible chips. The Malt & Hops is our favourite pub for its open fire and unpretentious attitude.

HUGO: If there's need to celebrate anything at all, then it's martinis on the terrace of the Ocean Mist (a hotel on a boat directly opposite Bard). It gives you a view all the way up to Edinburgh Castle, which is wonderful in August for enjoying the fireworks. And then either a smoked sausage supper from Pierinos if we're feeling dirty, or a fancier tasting menu at Heron on extra special occasions. Heron was awarded a Michelin star last year (the third restaurant in Leith, remarkably). All of this is within a five-minute radius of Bard and our home. How lucky we are.

Somewhere in Scotland to stray?

JAMES: We escape to Eilean Shona once a year. We adore Ness (Vanessa Branson). She has done wonderful things there to create and preserve the magic. We had our honeymoon in the Old Schoolhouse over Christmas and new year. We were the only souls on the island, and we were off grid with a lot of our wedding wine and whisky to get through. It was 2019/2020 so just pre-Covid. A hallowed time in a hallowed place.

HUGO: I'm from Skye and find the tug to return ever greater. Mountains, sea, midges – they're in my blood.

CUSTOMS
WHARF

Exhibitions, Events,
Studios, Hot Desks,
Workshop, Café, Shop.

Bard

Quine & Loon Cottage

BANCHORY, ABERDEENSHIRE

———

Aunty Core

Since 1860 this tiny granite cottage has housed farmers working in the adjacent steading. Today, it's home to a handbag designer who returned home to Aberdeenshire from London to be closer to her family and a quieter life. Swapping PowerPoint for power tools, owner Rachel Dougherty. has taken this cottage back to the bones and rebuilt it from the inside out – with a little help from her dad.

It's a family affair here, with two little nieces front and centre of its design, inspiring much of the owner's 'aunty core' aesthetic. Playful references ranging from Scottish folk, punk, bubblegum pop and country and western to a dash of Hello Kitty were added to the kaleidoscopic moodboard that gave birth to this designer abode. To walk into this storybook cottage, inspired by the pages of Rachel's favourite childhood fairytales, is to climb the beanstalk, taste the porridge and fall down a rabbit hole of colour, pattern and a healthy dose of fun.

This fairytale didn't start off as bright. Inside, the cottage was in bad shape with mould, damp, woodworm, rot and no insulation. Over one dusty year, Rachel and her dad returned the building to stone after years of questionable renovations, revealing a footprint that, with some clever design decisions, makes use of every square inch. Hidden storage, a hallway utility area and a niche shower practically (and joyfully) fill every crack and corner of this small yet mighty home.

Unafraid of hard graft and driven by her ever-dwindling budget, Rachel enrolled in a tiling course, sought wallpapering advice from her uncle, who is a painter and decorator, and watched YouTube videos to fill in the gaps.

Banchory is close to the Granite City of Aberdeen, so called for the stone much of the city is built in, but Rachel was adamant she would avoid its silvery tones as well as obvious farmhouse tropes. Instead, she created a cosy cottage with bright and cheery colours to get her through the long winter months. The only surface that hasn't been treated to a lick of colour is the tongue and groove panelling in the sitting room. Elsewhere, chequerboard tiles clash with ticking stripes, florals, gingham, tartan and unexpected flashes of red to create a confident scheme that feels both quiet and riotous, like a warm shortbread with popping candy inside.

To furnish her cottage, Rachel used as much second-hand, pre-loved, vintage, antique and handmade items as possible to save money, making best friends with local vintage and antique shopkeepers, and using Facebook Marketplace, eBay and Etsy. Obsessed with materials and textiles, she embraced vintage fabrics to make all her own soft furnishings. Although newly acquired, every piece in this home feels like an heirloom and perhaps with all the family memories being made here, they will become just that. But don't be fooled, while the home trades on nostalgia it feels modern and considered, only something your cool aunt who lived in London could pull off.

The biggest challenge on this project has been cost. The price of materials skyrocketed over the course of the renovation so plans for an extension and new kitchen are on hold, but Rachel remains philosophical. Only once she moved in did Rachel realise what she would really like from her new (old) home. It has taught her patience and that good things, like a hearty slow-cooked stew, take time. Until then, Rachel is happy to coorie in with her two nieces and her cat Drizzy, and make the occasional brew for her dad when he pops in to help with the next job on her list.

Small, awkward spaces have been turned into functional and stylish nooks.

*Left: check mates up with
rose and ticking stripe
wallpaper in the bathroom.
Right: timber panelling
and a clash of fabrics sing
harmoniously in the wee
sitting room.*

Q&A with Rachel Dougherty

___

What was your approach to designing the space?

Focusing on one room at a time, researching and sourcing, then creating moodboards to see if everything meshed together. I also wanted to be inspired by pieces of furniture or decor I've found and collected along the way.

Favourite elements you brought to the space?

First I'm really happy that the cottage was gutted and put back together again, so it's dry, warm and safe. Splitting the kitchen into two new rooms, the utility and a shower room, which adjoins the master bedroom. Last, but most importantly, I love the playful element I've added to this little old cottage. While I've tried to keep things traditional I have had fun with colour and pattern, adding character to something that was unloved.

How did the collaboration work between owner, architect and builder?

It was important that I found folk that understood my style and the fact that I wanted to use as much that was reclaimed and vintage as possible. Both the architect and contractor were amazing, we worked really closely together and they totally got my vision, which made the whole journey really enjoyable.

Design muse?

New Tolsta, the home of Tom Hickman. It's incredible. Completely unique and filled to the brim with character and joy.

Favourite spot to enjoy what you've created?

Probably the living room on my cosy sofa. I can look out at the incredible view, which usually includes the cows, as well as enjoying all the tat I've collected from hours spent searching charity shops as well as antique and vintage fairs.

Dream Scottish house guest?

The comedian Limmy! He's a daftie and we could have a laugh and eat calamari.

Who is spinning on the record player?

Sierra Ferrell and Cleo Sol.

House drink?

Mezcal margs.

Somewhere close to play?

Fish Shop in Ballater: beautiful decor and incredible food made with sustainably sourced seafood and local produce.

Somewhere in Scotland to stray?

Luskentyre Beach, Isle of Harris. Possibly the most beautiful place in the whole wide world.

Ballone Castle

TARBAT, EASTER ROSS

———

Contemporary Castle

This may be Scotland's biggest fixer-upper; it was left roofless after a rebellion in 1745 and continued to be neglected for nearly 200 years. By the mid-19th century it had lost much of its fine detail. Saved in the nick of time: a few years later and there may not have been much left to warrant a restoration.

This butter-toned fortress was rescued from ruin by can-do couple, Lachlan and Annie Stewart. They happened upon the windswept shell, inhabited by cows, on their mission to find a castle to call their family home. The couple always fancied living in a castle and one day, armed with MacGibbon and Ross's *The Castellated and Domestic Architecture of Scotland* and an Ordnance Survey map, they started looking. There was no road to Ballone so they had to walk across a field to get to where it sat on a clifftop overlooking the North Sea towards Norway.

After the couple convinced the local farmer to let them buy it, along with 12 acres, they set about doing it up. It took over 10 years for this warm and characterful home to emerge, with lime-washed walls in shades of pale ochre, sage green and iron oxide creating a light and airy feeling.

The castle's history has been animated once again with vaulted ceilings, beams made from Douglas fir struck by lightning on a nearby estate and a hearth that can accommodate a roaring fire (while underfloor heating and modern technology make things a little more comfortable for 21st-century living). The huge, double height 17th-century hall was restored in Arts and Crafts fashion and is their favourite space, the scene of family get-togethers and any excuse to throw a party. Looking out over the sea, this room gives the feeling of being on a ship.

From its very beginning, this has been a family affair. If buying a ruined castle and raising children on a building site wasn't enough, the couple launched their family-run interiors business ANTA at the same time, creating furnishing, textiles and stoneware inspired by the Scottish landscape and seasons. Mirroring the ethos of their business, Ballone is decorated with natural materials, with a collection of early Scottish furniture and ceramics, punctuated by stone and wood sourced locally, softened with hardy tweed and soft merino throws and cushions.

ANTA's trademark tartans are the perfect foil to these simple – but beautiful – pieces of furniture. Nothing in the home is exaggerated or over the top. 'That would not be in keeping with the castle,' says Annie.

Hidden passages reveal themselves, turning this home into an endless adventure.

We're great believers in the William Morris philosophy of owning pieces that are either beautiful or useful, and preferably both. Nothing is just an objet d'art.

Buttery plaster walls and ANTA woolen throws create a transition from medieval castle to warm, modern abode.

Left: timber clad
bathrooms are a signature
of the architect while a
thin metal staircase is
a modern, sculptural
intervention (right).

Inverlonan

GLENLONAN, OBAN

———

New Bothy

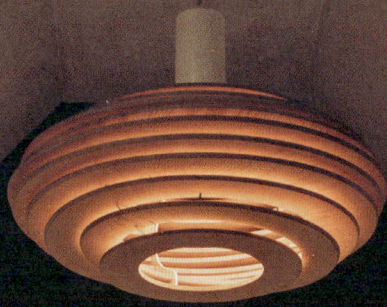

A bothy is typically a small hut or cottage used as a mountain refuge or shelter for shepherds. Effectively stone tents, these modest dwellings dot the remote landscape of the Highlands and islands.

Neolithic stones lead to the Inverlonan bothies. 'Inver' describes the area around the mouth of a river – in this case, the River Lonan. These bothies sit on Loch Nell under the shade of a gnarly oak tree and resident golden eagles, hen harriers and merlins.

The simple, architecturally driven, off-grid bothies are embedded in nature and intended as a modern re-imagining of the traditional bothy experience. Designed by social enterprise The Bothy Project, the prefabricated contemporary cabins were created for simplicity and seclusion.

First created as an artist's studio and sanctuary for creatives, the design sought to provide a space for solitude and self-reflection. Its compact size and pared-back aesthetic are a way to minimise distractions and help artists focus on the task at hand.

The owner of Inverlonan, Lupi Moll, has curated a premium, 'slow-living' hospitality experience with the bothies as the star attraction. 'When I got hold of the family farm at Inverlonan, I wanted to create an environmentally focused agri-tourism business that would make the most of this amazing site. I camped here as a Scout when I was about 12 years old and I remember thinking that there is something magical about this ancient oak woodland on the edge of the loch.'

To start with he planted about 200 acres of trees and then set about installing the first two bothies, Uisge and Beatha. These were followed by a third, Sitheil, and a wood-fired sauna.

To create this off-grid eco-experience it was important for Lupi to be true to nature and create structures that would sit well within the existing natural surroundings, selecting cladding options that would blend in with the bracken and trees, helping to ground them in their settings. 'I also appreciated the historic link to bothies as simple places of refuge.'

When going to a bothy, it is important to assume that there will be no facilities. No tap, no sink, no beds, no lights and, even if there is a fireplace, perhaps nothing to burn. Bothies may have a simple sleeping platform, but if busy you might find that the only place to sleep is on a stone floor.
Mountain Bothy Association

Local joiners have crafted a camp kitchen with a fire outside inviting dwellers to embrace the elements.

Above left: black clay plaster walls frame the loch views beyond. Above right: a mix of modern and vintage furniture elevate the camping experience to a home among the oak trees.

A striking and sensitive design, the bothies are beautifully thought out and their simplicity matches the simplicity of what Lupi is trying to achieve at Inverlonan. A gabled form recalling typical agricultural structures allows the bothies to sit quietly in any setting, while the precise lines of the corrugated metal and timber cladding introduce a contemporary edge. Inside, the unobstructed floor area makes optimal use of the available space, with a raised mezzanine bed, compact kitchen and seating area and windows on all aspects to provide plenty of natural light.

Beatha has black corrugated cladding, Sitheil a rusted corrugated cladding and for Uisge, Lupi sourced raised-seam, Corten steel cladding. The Corten steel and wooden bothy connects with the surrounding nature, making it as striking as it is sensitive to the environment it floats in. Intimate, thoughtful and warm, this simple shelter immerses you in the landscape. Without the distractions of everyday life, it offers a tranquil space that encourages anyone who inhabits it to slow down, recharge and reconnect with nature.

The bothies have been fitted with the highest quality natural furnishings and finishes. The 'rough luxury' aesthetic is best displayed in its clay plaster finish. This rough clay has been applied on the walls and ceilings and, as well as being a natural material, allows the building to breathe while absorbing toxins and passively regulating the temperature.

We bought the shell and I worked with a team of builders to install them on the tricky sites. Because they're off-grid, they sit on a ring beam that is anchored using simple ground screws. This minimises any impact on the environment and means they could be moved, if necessary, in the future.

A loft bed space tucked into the eaves is reached by a hidden ladder and creates the feeling of a luxury (and dry) tent.

Q&A with Lupi Moll

What was your approach to designing the space?

Embedded in nature, the landscape and local craftsmanship but with a light touch; we want to be able to remove the structures without a trace or lasting impact.

Favourite elements you brought to the space?

Clay walls for texture and light – especially the black demi-rustic clay with straw through it in Sitheil bothy. Local ash crafted by skilled local craftsmen into bothy tables, benches, kitchen pieces and ladders. Framed views out of all the windows – they're stunning in all seasons!

Design muse?

Frank Lloyd Wright.

Favourite spot to enjoy what you've created?

A bobbing boat on the loch.

Who is spinning on the record player?

There is silence. It's all about slow living, disconnecting, getting back to basics, immersing yourself in nature, all in ecological luxury. Embrace the pace. It takes time to light a fire, boil the kettle, hand-grind the coffee, but having been made with thought, effort and time it tastes that much better.

Dream Scottish house guest?

Alexander Selkirk, the Scottish sailor and inspiration for Robinson Crusoe.

What are you serving?

Anything from our farm, our land and our efforts. The freshest, most local, most seasonal, most ethically sourced ingredients we can find. Farm to fork.

Somewhere close to play?

Iona – crystal waters, white sands, history and astonishing natural beauty.

Somewhere in Scotland to stray?

Garden of Cosmic Speculation, a 30-acre sculpture garden by theorist and architect Charles Jencks. It is a celebration of nature and the senses. Nature in art.

Lamb's House

LEITH

———

Mary & Merchants

Leith was Scotland's chief port for centuries, trading across the North Sea and south to France, the Low Countries, the Mediterranean, the Baltic and the Americas, with ships carrying coal, grain, fish, juniper and hides and returning with spices, cloth, whale oil and wine.

The site here was originally owned by Edinburgh shipowner Andrew Lamb and today is one of the finest surviving examples of a merchant's house in Scotland. The 16th-century house, once visited by Mary Queen of Scots, has been restored and reborn and a deceptively new garden pavilion has been added, saving the house from its fate as a day centre for the elderly.

When owners Nick Groves-Raines and Kristin Hannesdottir took it on, the first port of call was to remove all the inappropriate modern interventions before they could rebuild. Lamb's House was a shadow of its 17th-century self, lost under its many guises over the years. There was a lift shaft stuck onto the back, a public hall extension built in 1960 at the front, raised doorways – and a brittle building across all five floors. In the process of bringing this structure back to life they kickstarted a renewed creative culture in the port town of Leith, more famous for *Trainspotting* than garden pavilions.

Despite having suffered many ill-fitting alterations over its long life, the form and essential character of the house remained intact and many of its original features survive today. These include the stone turnpike stair, fireplaces, slop sinks and most of the original pine beams.

Internally the house is fairly simple, with plastered walls, timber or plaster ceilings, timber floors, doors and leaded windows. Siberian larch was used for the roof timbers, handmade Hungarian glass for the windows and antique Swedish pantiles for the roof. All were chosen to be as similar to the original materials as possible.

Salvaged materials were used throughout, on the stone floors, worktops, sinks and taps. Sheep's wool insulation was used and materials were sourced locally where possible; all the ironmongery, latches, handles, hinges, nails, handrails and gates were made by a local blacksmith.

The slop sinks on each landing were unblocked, doors were lowered and fireplaces reopened. The trademark half-shuttered windows were reinstated and some 400 years after Lamb's House was built, it somehow feels as contemporary as the day it was born.

*We're in a building that was built
in 1610 and yet it works better now
than it probably ever did.*

A generous dining table
plays hosts to neighbours
and diplomats.

This approach – to incorporate the contemporary among the venerable – is apparent throughout Lamb's House: a Georgian mirror here, a Florentine chest of drawers there, a bold oil painting of a silver bowl on an unframed canvas (the latter done by Kristin herself). The kitchen table, a former laundry table retrieved from Holyrood, anchors the home and is a gathering space for the whole community.

One of the most surprising elements of the home, the garden, is only eight years old. Within the new walls of this oasis in the city sits an 18th-century-inspired pavilion with an ogee roof. The romantic little building was the last on the site and took three years to be completed.

It took a family of conservation architects (alongside their son Gunnar, Nick and Kristin run GRAS architects) and a cast of builders led by their son-in-law to act as architect, developer and main contractor on the restoration project, an enterprising spirit the merchants of days gone by would respect. The new and existing buildings are now used as a home and studio for the family business, exactly as was the case in the early 17th century when it was the home and business premises of Andrew Lamb.

Left: an oxblood four-poster bed anchors the sleeping quarters. Right: a spiral stone staircase runs through the bowels of the building and into a lofty bedroom and bathroom.

Above: a box bed provides
cosy quarters in the
pavilion. Right: a grand
sitting room leads into a
library and snug in the
main house.

Kyle House

TONGUE, SUTHERLAND

———

Modern Age

A former drover's cottage, Kyle House is a uniquely Scottish dwelling with a Scandinavian sensibility. The derelict building was meticulously restored using traditional materials and techniques, marrying contemporary design with its wild setting to create a home that sits still, even when it's blowing a hooley outside.

Approaching the humble building, a frameless gable window is the first hint at its contemporary intervention. Push open the heavy oak door and you will find a refined, almost monastic interior.

A series of oak-lined boxes have been carefully placed inside its solid stone structure, with all windows offering wild views beyond. In the living room, cosily next to the log-burning stove, a window seat reading nook looks out towards the sea and Kyle of Tongue. While eating breakfast in the kitchen you can overlook the dramatic Ben Loyal, a four-peaked Corbett, or from the bathtub upstairs soak in the splendour of the Highlands in all their glory.

This wild hideaway sits in solitude amid raw Scottish nature. The interior itself is an invitation to retreat, contemplate and embrace a slower pace of life. In contrast to the ruggedness outside, there is a fine detail throughout, from the carefully crafted Danish oak kitchen to the bespoke joinery.

Natural materials hewn from the landscape set the tone. Architects GRAS have tried to select only the most necessary items, and ensure that those they do select are truly special. Oak-lined walls and an open plan mean that Kyle can be whatever its dwellers want it to be – a romantic getaway for two, or a retreat in the wild for one.

It was a highly collaborative approach responding to Wildland's vision for the project with GRAS working very closely with Ruth Kramer, the owners, and Ewen MacRae, the builder, as well as a host of other specialist craftspeople.

We were collectively committed to create a beautiful, quiet and serene space nestled within the faithfully restored historic shell. Our intervention sought to explore and celebrate the very best of Scottish and Scandinavian ideas, craftsmanship and materials in a way that would stand the test of time, perhaps even improving with use.

A quiet palette of oak, plaster and natural fabrics create a contemplative place to be in nature.

With very little remaining of the original interior, the plan was reinterpreted and rationalised to form a series of equally proportioned living spaces. These spaces are formed by finely detailed oak inserts placed into the lime-plastered shell of the remaining stone structure, defining living areas within and between them. Importantly, space is given in equal measure to sleeping, eating, living and bathing. Everything is constructed using a simple material palette of stone, heart oak, lime plaster, brass, leather and glass. Technology is used only where it supports easy and efficient living in the house.

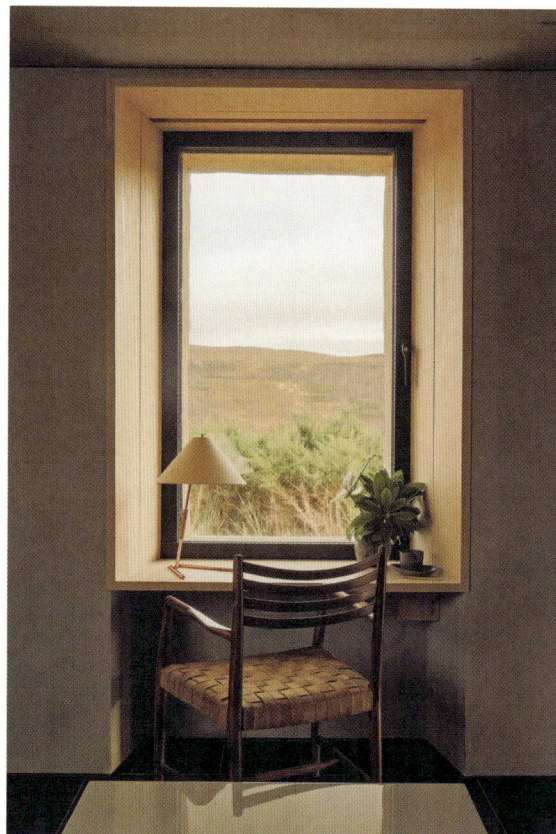

Oak joinery frames views into the landscape beyond.

A log burning stove and window nook invite you to sit within the landscape.

Q&A with Gunnar Groves-Raines, architect

Design muse?

My wife, Dieny Itoe, Creative Director at Custom Lane and fashion designer by training, is a constant source of inspiration and motivation, as well as constructive criticism. We are so fortunate to be able to explore places and spaces together and it is one of my greatest pleasures to see her enjoy things that we have helped to create.

Favourite spot to enjoy what you've created?

In the middle of summer, the sun sets in the far north over the Kyle of Tongue, a tidal estuary which runs out over sandbanks to the north Atlantic and the islands beyond the Kyle. I could sit in the living space in front of the fire enjoying that north view for hours. Kyle House is the only dwelling with this incredible view. In winter, Ben Loyal morphs from a beautiful hill to a dramatic mountain and the view of it changes from one minute to the next as weather passes through. The head of the bath is perfectly aligned for this dramatic scene, especially on colder snowy days.

Who is spinning on the record player?

Whenever I've had the pleasure of staying at Kyle, much of the time has been in silence, or in close conversation. The architecture is deliberately quiet and restrained, designed to support connection with the landscape around, and it often feels like anything more could disturb that. Only after dark, or perhaps while cooking or making a morning coffee, would I be tempted to put anything on.

Dream Scottish house guest?

Having spent hundreds of hours as a child driving in the Highlands listening to his shows recorded on tape, Billy Connolly would be a very easy choice. Some of the most enriching dinners I've had in the north have been with locals who have incredible stories (including ghost stories) and folklore of the area.

House drink?

Perhaps a glass of well-chosen wine from the Wildland cellar with food, otherwise perhaps a Feragaia sour, to best support early morning walks or even a swim in the river below the house.

Somewhere close to play?

Many fun nights have been had in the Ben Loyal Hotel with both locals and visitors for company, especially when someone picks up one of the many instruments casually left lying around.

Somewhere in Scotland to stray?

Dun Mahaig broch (roundhouse), just a few hundred metres away on a ridge to the west, is an ancient (2,500-year-old) structure that still has many of its original features intact. It's rumoured that Kyle House was built from stone salvaged from the broch.

Kilmartin Castle

KILMARTIN, ARGYLL

———

Thrifty Castle

An Aussie and a Geordie walked into a Scottish castle with a 'for sale' sign out front and the Geordie girl said, 'Okay, never mind, at least it was a pretty drive.' The Australian said, 'Holy cow, this is bloody awesome, we can absolutely do this.'

Once upon a time, around the Ice Age, the valley of Kilmartin was carved out by the melting of glaciers. Sitting proudly above the prehistoric glen of Kilmartin, the 16th-century castle stronghold is covered in modern art, vintage signs and cinema posters. From Iron Age to New Age, knights have been replaced by Pac-Man statues guarding the stairs, a pull-down cinema screen and a portrait of a bearded man in a dress.

It was a long journey to get to this point for owners Stef Burgon and Simon Hunt, first living in another country and then camping on the grounds, working as apprentice builders on the castle makeover. Having spent all their money buying the castle, albeit at a bargain basement price for a ruin, Stef and Simon had no choice but to become their own builders, doing much of the work themselves, learning to pay attention to materials.

Their first port of call was repainting, everywhere. It took 120 litres of paint and they did it while off work one Easter weekend, with only show tunes on the radio for company. It was their first castle test, of many.

Old stone buildings need airflow. As soon as we got the front door and the windows open, and had people in and out creating airflow, it started to breathe. The door had been shut for around 10 years, it was damp and musty. We did a very basic upgrade to begin with because we were living 4,884 miles away in Dubai, had full-time jobs, and needed to pop it on the holiday rental market to 'wash its face'. We would periodically travel to the castle with art from our studio apartment that we had collected over the years and Persian rugs we bought from local souks, slowly adding a bit of us into the building.

A dining room tucked into the cellar is illuminated by statement lighting and candles.

This castle sits amid one of the UK's most important archaeological sites, akin to a Scottish Stonehenge. For almost 500 years it has stood at the top of the ancient Argyll glen, surrounded by standing stones, hill forts, rock carvings and burial cairns – more than 800 archaeological monuments.

It was built in 1550 by the rector of Kilmartin Church, John Carswell, who spread Christianity through the isles, and who may have had a thing or two to say about its new owners' taste in art. The castle then belonged to the Campbell clan for 200 years before falling into ruin from 1790 and being rescued in the 90s by a couple who would go on to create two bedrooms and a bathroom in this family bolthole. Enter our new king and queen Simon and Stef, who would go on to ensure this remains no ordinary Scottish castle. New heating and plumbing, roof repairs and a new kitchen followed, but it is the bits in between that excite this intrepid couple, who have left no stone unturned, both inside and outside the castle.

From outside, this moody castle looms large and at night, its walls are illuminated theatrically, with tiny glowing windows and conical towers bookending it. Inside, it feels like a home, albeit the home of your eclectic cousins. There are no painted ceilings, chandeliers or tartan-bedecked walls. Instead, this storybook castle has been imaginatively restored, laced with modern verve. It took a long time to get to this point with vaulted ceilings, copper tubs and a wild swimming pond.

Paint has been a big consideration for this colourful couple, understanding that the lime-rendered walls of the castle needed to breathe. They fell in love with eco-friendly lime paints, which create a soft, matte and romantic finish. The high pH balance also makes it near-impossible for mould to live on. They fell so hard they have since started working on their own lime paint company.

The furniture and objects throughout the castle are all antiques they collected over time, from a modular vintage sofa they picked up in Poland to pine settles that have been cut up and put back together again to create window reading nooks.

This modern medieval castle handsomely rests in Kilmartin Glen.

We believe in the buy well, buy once approach, regardless of your budget. Ours was not huge. We spent a lot of time researching and considering how things would age and look with a little wear.

It is clear that Stef and Simon love antiques of all eras. Things made so well in their day that they can still be enjoyed now. When they do buy new, they ask themselves, 'Will this survive and get better with age? Would we buy it in 60 years if we stumbled across it in an antique store?' They carried this design principle throughout, using reclaimed encaustic floor tiles in the bathrooms, investing in new antique-style brass toggle light switches, and concrete pouring their own kitchen worktops, which are happily imperfect.

Every nook and cranny has been used in this space, from a grandfather clock that hides pipes going up a wall to a small stone store that has been transformed into a library, with club chair and record player. Plants, lamps, rugs and blankets, bar carts, vintage radios and a tongue-in-cheek approach to decorating make this feel like home.

Furnishing the castle was such an enjoyable process. One of our favourite things to do is hiring a BIG van, driving to Newark Fair, and being at the entrance gate, torch in hand, at 6am.

Far left: Pac Man figures guard the stairwell. Left: a four-poster wrought iron bed is calling, after a soak in the copper tub fit for a king and queen (right).

Q&A with Simon Hunt and Stef Burgon

Favourite addition to the space?

The Bearded Lady, who takes pride of place in the grand hall, in the spot where typically an oil painting of the laird would hang. She spent her early life, in the 1920s, hanging in the reception of Parisian hot-spot members' hangout, The Castel Club – frequented by folks like Andy Warhol, David Bowie, and Keith Haring. We like to think of her as having left the club scene behind, retiring to this cosy Scottish castle, and enjoying slightly more peace and quiet. She was bought at auction before Stef understood what a 'buyer's premium' was. We won and lost that auction simultaneously as the hammer landed and it dawned on us that we had paid almost a third more than we thought we had. Luckily, this lesson happened at the beginning of the build before we knew how much the plumbing was going to cost. She's part of the family now and we can't imagine the grand hall without her.

As a couple, how did the collaboration work?

Stef does not excel at this. Stef is happy to give up on an idea if unsure of it herself, but if she loves it, SHE WILL FIGHT TO THE DEATH to have it. This is her understanding of collaboration.

Design muse?

In an odd way, Dubai was our counter-muse. We were so used to being surrounded by modernity that we were craving all things old. Anything that had a story to tell appealed. Objects made by hand and not machine felt like they held an energy. Being surrounded by new made us appreciate the character of old.

Favourite spot to enjoy what you've created?

On a crisp spring morning we like to sit in the glasshouse overlooking the wild swimming pool and the glen beyond. There are views back to the castle from what was once a boggy field. We used to sit at the top of the garden during the build and eat lunch in between back-breaking jobs. Sitting there now makes it all feel worthwhile. When it comes to projects, the garden was as hard as the castle.

Who is spinning on the record player?

One of the first records we played in the grand hall was 'Home Again' by Michael Kiwanuka and whenever we hear a song from the album it takes us straight there. At that time the fire didn't work properly and would blow smoke into the room every time the wind blew, all we had were board games for entertainment and a rickety sofa that the previous owners, Tom and Olive, had left behind when they sold up. It's quite emotional just thinking about that time. We knew the castle had the bones to be incredible but it is so much better today than we could have ever imagined.

Dream Scottish house guest?

John Carswell. The castle was built for this important religious chap in 1550 and we would love to have him back here to see what he thinks of the upgrades. We reckon he would be impressed by the underfloor heating, grateful for the bespoke padding on low lintels, and there probably wasn't a 16th-century copper bath he could soak in back then, being seven foot tall. Ideally though, we would like to be the guests and have him plan an evening menu, accompanied by his favourite music in the grand hall for us.

What are you serving?

That's got to be a hearty venison stew from the hillside, with rowan berry jelly, sweet shallots and Grandma's carrots grown in the organic garden. This incredibly lean, free-range, organic meat was never on our radar. Back in the 90s in Newcastle, we weren't exactly feasting on venison – more likely to find a few noble fish and chips than a plate of fancy deer meat. It was even rarer on a family farm in Bordertown, Australia, so neither of us had tried it until we moved to Scotland.

Somewhere close to play?

On a sunny day, we catch the ferry to Gigha (which is Viking for 'the fair isle'), hop off the other side and walk along the beach with our shoes off to The Boathouse for mackerel ceviche, Boathouse bunny chow, which is a must-try seafood curry, and Machrihanish brown crab. Then jump off the pier into the crystal blue waters before heading back to the castle for a local whisky by the fire.

Somewhere in Scotland to stray?

There is a secret spot, down a forest path, opposite a lochside mill, and an intimidating jump over a stream, where at the right time of year the ground becomes a golden carpet of chanterelle mushrooms. We like to stray there for a forager's reward. Everybody in the Scottish countryside has a 'secret spot'.

Old Duloch House

DUNFERMLINE, FIFE

———

Blessed are the Cheesemakers

Built in 1729, this house and garden sits among new estates and highways today but was once surrounded by farmland, kings and parliament.

Just a short drive from Edinburgh over the Queensferry Crossing lies the ancient borough of Dunfermline in Fife. From the reign of King Malcolm III and Queen Margaret in the mid-11th century, the town became the seat of power and capital of Scotland, remaining so until the brutal murder of James I in Perth in 1437, when administrative power and capital status were passed to Edinburgh.

Robert the Bruce is buried in the abbey here alongside six kings, two queens and three princes, known as the forgotten monarchs. More recently, the area has given rise to Scottish punk bands The Skids and Nazareth and two rebellious cheesemongers.

Old Duloch is a Georgian mansion house that was for a short while the main house on the estate, only to be replaced and filled with farm workers after a new house was built in 1844. By the 1960s it would become derelict, later to be restored by its new custodians, Iain and Karen Mellis.

Their eponymous I.J. Mellis cheesemongers are traditional shops, with old-fashioned service selling artisan farmhouse cheese. In May 1993, Iain opened his first outpost, locating a small, damp, cave-like shop halfway up Victoria Street, the now famous winding cobblestone lane in Edinburgh's Old Town. It was an ideal location that could be kept cool and damp without too much trouble – perfect for storing cheese.

Inspired by cheese cellars, it is the cool and dark basement that perhaps has undergone the most significant work at Old Duloch House. Taking out the fitted kitchen, Iain and Karen discovered a large fireplace. Knocking through the dividing wall between the library and the kitchen made it one large kitchen with a relaxed sitting area. The couple added brick

tiles to both rooms and the corridor to create a more robust space that gives the feeling of a servants' kitchen that would look right at home 300 years ago.

None of the new cabinetry is fitted; instead, old furniture acts as benchtop and storage, as it would originally have done. A handsome cooker heats and nourishes its owners, while a tall island is the perfect grazing station. A larder and entrance house the fridge and preparation spaces. The home's most modern element, Crittall doors, separate the kitchen and dining library. Creating a sightline but allowing two toasty spaces makes the most of this narrow basement area.

An industrial-sized excavation of woodchip wallpaper was the first priority in tackling this house. Upstairs, the drawing room's original panelled walls have been scraped back and years of paint has been peeled and revealed, with the patina confirming this couple very much prefers old over new.

Like the Egyptians, Greeks and Romans before them, they have hung wall tapestries generously throughout the space, not just for decoration but rather cleverly to hide the sins of the building or renovations gone by.

The floors have been softened with rush matting. Handwoven, plaited, coiled and stitched, the rush feels respectful of the building's age and modern all at once, adding a natural, calm and cohesive feeling across all the spaces. The rooms are filled with antiques older than the home: oil paintings, statues of saints, linens and taxidermy – all sourced mostly during cheese-buying trips across the UK.

The last job has been lining the attic rooms with wood and bringing them back to period with the furnishings. Much of the brown furniture is French and has been picked up at auctions – with Iain adding antiquing to his fromage obsession.

Chunky sisal carpet creates a contemporary soft touch to this storied space.

Panelling has been stripped of paint with a romantic petina remaining, contrasting with the rich oak settle and dining table.

*A lifetime's collection of
art, objects and auction
finds brings the walls and
niches to life.*

Q&A with Karen Mellis

What was your approach to designing the space?

We endeavoured to bring the house back to its period after it fell into disrepair and was renovated in the 1960s. There was a lot of paring back to the original walls and floor, stripping out the fitted kitchen and bathrooms, and replacing with items of a natural simplicity.

As a couple, how did the collaboration work?

As a couple we think we collaborate on projects pretty well, all things considered. This is probably borne out of many years working professionally together relatively successfully (at I.J. Mellis Cheese). We each have our different strengths (and weaknesses), and we're pretty in tune with each other's thoughts, most of the time.

Design muse?

Restoration House Rochester, Dennis Severs' house in London and a little B&B in Carmarthen, Wales called Dorian's Place.

Favourite spot to enjoy what you've created?

The house is generally quite a cool house and during the winter months, we need to be where the wood burners are, so a large part of our time is spent in the kitchen and adjoining library and dining area. However, in the summer months the sitting room can be quite warm and bright as it has windows to the south and west. Iain says he likes the tiny bathroom as it's the only warm place in the house.

Who is spinning on the record player?

Luckily we're old enough to have lots of records from years ago, but Joni Mitchell at Carnegie Hall is the flavour of the month.

Dream Scottish house guest?

Sam Heughan, who plays Jamie in the period drama *Outlander*. It would be rude not to invite Caitríona Balfe, who plays his screen wife Clare. Despite the drama, both have a dry sense of humour.

What are you serving?

Mince on sourdough toast, a regular plate of food put down to us at Granny's. Perhaps served with a watercress salad to update it a bit.

Somewhere close to play?

Culross and Falkland, both relatively similar with impressive palace walls adorned in tapestries with amazing gardens in the centre of historic villages – very relaxing, but inspirational, places to unwind.

Somewhere in Scotland to stray?

They say Inverness is the gateway to the Highlands, so this would be the place to start an exploratory journey of beauty into Scotland. It's also where we both met many years ago, so for us a place of fond memories as well.

Dun Guaidhre

ISLE OF MULL

———

Fisherman's Cottage

This stone cottage on the rocky north coast of Mull, in the middle of a field, overlooks the sea towards Coll and the small isles of Rum, Eigg and Muck in the Inner Hebrides. It has been a shelter for fishermen, sheep and hillwalkers all looking for refuge against the wild west coast weather.

Dun Guaidhre has stood for centuries next to the remains of an ancient Iron Age fort, or 'dun'. Although it remains unchanged outside, it has had a decidedly modern upgrade, kept deliberately as modest as it always has been.

It was important for architects Peter and Rachel Harford-Cross to retain the existing qualities of the cottage. Originally built as a simple family black house, typical of those all over the Hebrides, the cottage was nearly lost to ruin at the beginning of the 20th century but was saved for its use as a sheep byre. Later the sheep were moved out and it was made habitable again to provide basic shelter from the elements. Over the years many hands have added to and shaped this simple cottage, and their marks and interventions tell its history.

The owners and architects had a light-touch brief, focusing on simplicity and minimal intervention. Their challenge was to improve the fabric of the building without losing the basic, simple and open qualities of the space.

Budgetary reasons and a difficult site on a grassy plateau with no traditional vehicle access were two reasons for the brief, but the driving force was to create a space that was in keeping with the spirit and history of the simple dwelling, while making it robust and comfortable enough for modern needs.

It was important to preserve the existing character such as the bare stone walls, which received a plain whitewashed paint job, highlighting the deep walls that stand between the cosy space and the whipping Atlantic winds. The roof boards and beams remain unchanged, painted a light grey to reflect the typical Hebridean sky.

A cloakroom and a bathroom are the only separate spaces that were added here, behind plywood panelling. The ply was cut in irregular widths and constructed with a shadow gap to create the illusion of a hardwood boarded finish, but using this typically more affordable and lighter material. The oak and stone floor helps to anchor the space.

The living space and tiny kitchenette are concealed in a cupboard with a folding door. A generous bedroom has been cleverly zoned by a curtain and a second camping space or snug, just enough for two people, has been added above, accessible by a ladder.

Where materials were added they were done so sparingly and selected for longevity and quality.

The furniture and fittings were also carefully chosen with this approach in mind. The space has been fitted out with second-hand furniture, from the chairs to the reclaimed ship's light fittings to the bathroom sink, which was lying in a neighbouring shed. A wood-burning range in the living space is the sole means of cooking, providing warmth and hot water. More refined than rustic, the space feels quiet and reflective.

Whitewashed stone walls and an exposed ceiling create a deceptively light and open plan cottage.

We wanted to use little new material and, where possible, to use materials that were at hand and could be reused. This was partly due to the wish to be as sustainable as possible in the modern meaning of the word, but also as a continuation of the way this building had been simply and modestly adapted through its long life.

Above: plywood has been fashioned into panelling to honour its humble origins. Right: a simple kitchen has been tucked into a wall.

*Folding doors hide
functional areas like
this kitchenette artfully
concealed in a cupboard.*

Q&A with Peter and Rachel Harford-Cross

———

Three favourite elements you brought to the space?

1. The wood burning range stove. Not only does this provide warmth and a focal point to the space, it also has the capacity to heat water for bathing via the back boiler, or bake bread. You could be entirely self-sufficient and live off-grid if you choose to.

2. The reclaimed brass ship light fittings. Salvaged from scrapped merchant ships, these have an intrinsic solidity and character. The richness of the brass adds colour and warmth to the space.

3. The door latches. These brass fittings were designed and handmade specifically for the ledged and braced doors, very much in keeping with the spirit of the place.

How did the collaboration work between owner, architect and designer?

The work was done in a far less formal and structured way than larger projects, mainly due to its small scale and remote location. We employed a young craftsman more used to small joinery commissions who had never undertaken a project of this size, but showed great interest in the project and a willing spirit. We worked closely with him on site. Together, we discussed the design and this developed over time, sometimes by following his suggestions, sometimes by developing more organically, but always based on the initial design concept. This was only possible due to his skill and design eye and our willingness to work hands-on where necessary. This meant we could leave him to concentrate on areas where he could best bring his joinery skills to bear. The process was not always plain sailing and in the end the project took far longer than expected. At times this added a tension to the relationships and it was a credit to the client that she was patient throughout. Her trust in this process and faith that it would produce something that was truly worthy of the time and effort involved, was vital to see the project through to a successful conclusion.

Design muse?

The client's parents (the previous owners of the cottage), for their resourceful and creative approach to living on Mull when it was much less accessible and connected than it is today. Having lived through the tough war years and the true austerity of the 1950s, they thrived on making the best of the limited resources they had and using them in a creative way.

Favourite spot to enjoy what you've created?

Our favourite place to sit is in the new window seat at the west end of the building, which looks out to the Isle of Coll. In high summer the sun sets over the sea facing this window and the whole space is bathed in light.

Who is spinning on the record player?

Although we love music, part of the joy of the cottage is the great sense of calmness and quiet you feel in the space without any additional noise. We enjoy just listening to the noise of the wind and the fire in the stove.

House drink?

A gin and tonic with lime.

Dream Scottish house guest?

Robert Louis Stevenson, for his skill in telling a good adventure story on a dark and stormy night. His family also built many of the lighthouses around Scotland, including Ardnamurchan lighthouse, visible just round the headland.

Somewhere close to play?

The restaurant Croft 3 on the west side of Mull, for its delicious locally sourced food, wonderful views along the coast and its relaxed convivial atmosphere.

Somewhere in Scotland to stray?

We always enjoy a visit to the hills and countryside around the River Tweed, particularly at Bemersyde House. The landscape, with garden-like valleys, woods and rolling hills, resonate with Scotland's ancient past and mark a contrast with the west coast.

We wanted to preserve this character, reflecting all of its past uses. We therefore left the existing fabric untouched where it still functioned and only made alterations where they would make significant improvements.

Ferguson

GOVANHILL, GLASGOW

———

Tiny Tenement

From the street, this looks like a typical Glasgow tenement in the lively and creative suburb of Govanhill. Somewhere to stay, rather than live, it was imagined as a base for its owner and his creative friends to camp out, work and entertain.

Ferguson exists as a personal space from which to take part in the life of a neighbourhood, establishing social connections, supporting local businesses and participating in civic life.

The space emerged, over time, in all places, on WhatsApp between architect Lee Ivett, designer Simon Harlow and developer Duncan Blackmore. This 25 square metre apartment comprises a cramped hall and partition walls separating a shower, kitchen and sleeping area.

For Simon, the project is a spatial painting of sorts and an opportunity to design with his hands. For Lee, the project is about the pursuit of a formal language that encourages and responds to movement and occupation. For Duncan, the project is about the manifesting of a spatial experience imbued with the resources (including materials, skills and relationships) provided by an area of the city he is beginning to know well.

The main space is entirely unprogrammed and uncluttered and has almost nothing in it. You can use it for a meeting or a party or just as somewhere to sit and think. It is versatile and unfussy.

The main idea for the redesign was to create circulation, both on the ground and vertically, opening the space to reveal the four-metre-high ceiling. Duncan, the owner, wanted to be able to walk around the flat even though it is so tiny. As you walk through the green door, to an equally cheery yellow hall, you'll be greeted with the fun-size flat's curves, sharp lines and soaring ceilings.

Minimal furniture and doors create a free-flowing space, while geometric shapes and voids create playful energy alongside the vibrant colours. Bold primary colours enliven the space and the top half of the flat, where a mezzanine bed is drenched in a sunny saffron, is a reversal of the painted walls in the tenement's shared stairwell. The bed is reached via a set of wooden steps, with a small circular hole seen from the living area providing somewhere to place a hand while manoeuvring into position. Everything below is grey, to calm the space.

Constrained by its existing footprint, the team had to get creative. The shower room, which had been close to the front entrance, was shifted to the opposite side of the flat and became the only room closed off by a door. Its surfaces are swathed from top to bottom in blue and white Mirrl, a Japanese-inspired flecked polyester resin co-created by Simon and produced in Glasgow. It covers the entire space from floor to ceiling to shower tray to door, and gets its decorative flecks from paint scrapings saved from previous production runs of earlier Mirrl products.

Many items within the project were sourced extremely locally – sometimes even found on the street – or had been left over from previous projects. Material such as the oak for the bathroom door handle had been saved by Simon for 15 or more years. Very little was purchased or shipped from distant suppliers. Almost everything was made in a workshop a short walk away.

The taps, the lightbulbs and the cooker are the only items that were bought, ready-made, for the build. Practically everything else was created from scratch, from the red cast concrete sink to the sliding lock concealed inside the shower room's door.

This is a place to play, dream and stay, if only for a little while. There is a whole world outside to explore.

Walking through the front door, you are greeted with curves, sharp lines and soaring ceilings.

The project is extremely unusual in its approach to a design and making process, with collaboration and joint decision-making running the length of the build. Obstacles or failure were always absorbed and embraced as opportunities for enrichment rather than reduction or dilution. Simon is not only an incredible maker, but an accomplished artist.
Duncan Blackmore, owner

The uncluttered and unprogrammed main space is flexible enough to work rest and play, whatever the mood takes.

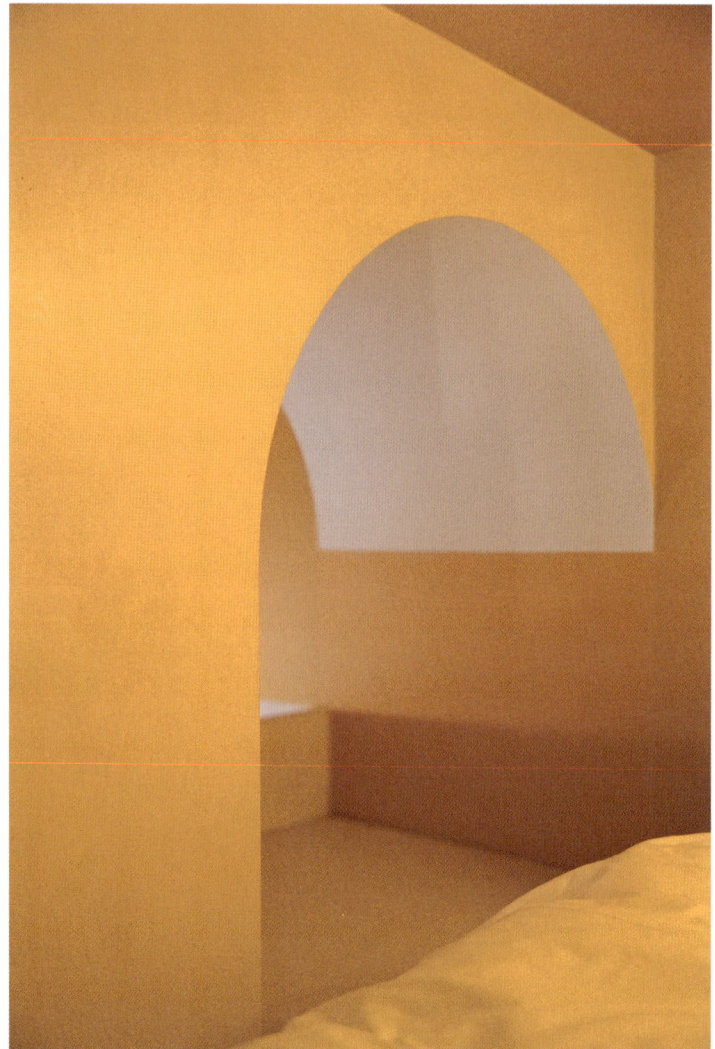

At 25m², the space is significantly below minimum space standards for new properties and is not intended as a self-contained, fully equipped home. Instead, it explores the potential of its position in a vital neighbourhood full of facilities and small businesses upon which the occupier can rely.

A cast sink was made on site (left) while playful curves create movement in the small space.

Q&A with Simon Harlow, designer and maker

———

Three favourite elements you brought to the space?

1. The red cast concrete sink, because a relatively mundane domestic fitting has been celebrated and elevated as a sculptural object in its own right, and in this case one that can be used from opposite ends – to wash your hands as you enter the flat on the hallway side, and as a normal sink for dishes on the kitchen side.

2. The bathroom door integrated handle and sliding lock mechanism, because it's a very neat way to perform two separate functions with a single fitting.

3. The 'halved cube' Mirrl 'Fossil' lining in the bathroom, because it makes a fully waterproof room and carries a light, almost stellar, pattern which is both invigorating and calming.

Design muse?

Björk.

Favourite spot to enjoy what you've created?

Sitting on the built-in bench.

Dream Scottish house guest?

Robert Stevenson (civil engineer).

Who is playing on the record player?

'Do Matter' by Plaid from the album *Digging Remedy*.

House drink?

Gin and tonic with ice and lime.

Somewhere close to play?

Outside the roll shop (Continental Deli) on Victoria Road, because it's right in the middle of the community, so you bump into loads of people and have good chats.

Somewhere in Scotland to stray?

The woods. Ideally mature deciduous or old growth pine forest, because in my view there is simply nowhere better than the woods!

Kinloch Lodge

BEN LOYAL, SUTHERLAND

———

Scandi Scot

Kinloch Lodge was once a private lodge for the Duke of Sutherland. Today, this handsome stone and wood building has been gently reimagined with an eclectic layering of pattern, textures and natural materials to create a series of spaces that are comfortably livable and casually curated.

The invitation to guests here is to 'stay where the world can't find you', hidden amongst dramatic mountains, wild rivers, pristine beaches, and never ending peatland in the far north of Scotland near the village of Tongue. 'Think noth, then go north a bit, and then keep going', explains Ruth Kramer, the interior designer responsible for its renovation. The landscape is a playground for wild swimming, trekking, cycling, fishing and climbing.

There is adventure to be had indoors too. Kinloch is a building that is likely to sweep you up and hold you in its warm embrace, whether that's getting lost in a book, cosying up in the library or feeling at one with nature in the conservatory, sheltered from the unpredictable weather.

'The wonderful thing about Kinloch as a series of spaces is the interplay between major and minor rooms, and how each serves a purpose,' says Ruth. It's an old sporting lodge, so large dining rooms and shared spaces are a given. But what makes the building truly special are the smaller nooks, like those with a roaring fire, or the cupboard with a handcrafted in-built desk – these are spaces to quietly withdraw and find calm.

The layout is something of a warren, with snaking, slightly narrow corridors and staircases helping those who come here to feel at home. It really is an interior that plays with scale. Outside, Kinloch retains much of its vernacular charm, including a delightful (and now quite rare) mix of harl, slated walls, and corrugated iron annexes. It comes together to create a perfectly imperfect collection of materials, which feels strongly of its place.

The restoration of Kinloch has happened very naturally, and very gradually. 'It has been a process of peeling back layers, trying new ideas, and seeing what feels good.' Creating these spaces has been a living, breathing process – art, objects and furniture are constantly being introduced to create a layered and genuine experience of home. 'In this respect, we have left the layout of the floorplan largely intact.'

One major intervention has been the orangery, crafted with great care by local hands and filled with green plants and wicker furniture. This space enjoys a unique view of Ben Loyal, and simultaneously feels open to the elements and intensely private.

The decoration is a more eccentric and more colourful take on 'Scandi Scot'. 'We have so many wonderful original features to work with, including the original V-line panelling and lots of well-worn carpentry. We've tried to put ourselves in the shoes of someone who might live here – perhaps an art collector with a taste for warm colours and deep, soft sofas.'

Highland heather, teals and silvery sky greys wash over the walls and work alongside playful artefacts and more refined Scandi furniture. Where she can, Ruth has tried to ensure that each room has a strong mix of textures, and that these work in tandem to create a feeling, rather than follow a style.

There is no competing with the ancient landscape that Kinloch Lodge rests upon, but the spaces here manage to successfully reflect its splendour.

The timber-clad annex is furnished in contemporary oak and decorated with old-school maps.

Elemental spaces combine stone and wood with fire to create cosy and inviting places to retreat.

Foggy florals and rich velvets create calm, cocooning bedrooms, echoing the rhythms of the surrounding landscape.

Q&A with Ruth Kramer, interior designer

What was your approach to creating this space?

I always want to put myself in the shoes of some imaginary muse when I think about a building. With Kinloch, we thought about it belonging to some wonderfully charming imaginary art collector. We took a very natural, slow approach to bringing this space together – filling it with objects, furniture, and art over a number of years. In this way, we hope the spaces feel genuine and welcoming – like visiting an old friend. We are much more concerned with creating a 'feeling' over following a style.

What inspires you?

My ideas always crystallise when I go walking in nature, where my mind is totally free and at its happiest. I take a lot of inspiration from what I find out there. I also devour books. I'm always inspired by conversations and interesting people – I find a good talk can start a chain reaction, and conjure new moods.

Favourite spot to enjoy what you've created?

I could sit in the conservatory each day and just look out and follow the wind, the sky and the rhythm of nature.

Who is spnning on the music player?

I do think the house is a place for quiet retreat… but sometimes Mozart's Clarinet Concerts with open doors and full volume are magic in a place like this.

Dream Scottish house guest?

If I could, Tilda Swinton. I would just sit and listen to all her stories of the people she's met and the places she's been, all while admiring her beauty.

House drink?

A favourite is sea buckthorn syrup with a dash of tonic and topped off with champagne. Nearly healthy, beautiful to look at, and a bit feminine.

Somewhere close to play?

Sorry, when I'm at Kinloch, I really like to make the most of the peace and quiet of the house. I'm far happier staying here with a good book and a warm fire.

Somewhere in Scotland to stray?

There are so many wonderful places to choose – there are hidden lochs, quiet woods and wide open spaces, but my very favourite place is Skinnet beach, where white sand and craggy rocks meet the sea. It's perfect for a walk on your own or an early morning swim.

Gairnshiel

RIVER GAIRN, ROYAL DEESIDE

———

Good Neighbours

Everybody needs good neighbours and Gairnshiel counts Balmoral Castle among theirs. Royals from Queen Victoria to King Georges V and VII have all stopped by, possibly to borrow a cup of sugar or perhaps to hunt for grouse in the hills surrounding the lodge. Built in 1746 and through its proceeding years, the Victorian hunting estate was kitted out in tartan carpets and pink walls. It was not until 2015, when a Belgian couple and their sons fell in love with the Highlands, that it got its most dramatic facelift – recast and refined. The owners, alongside Belgian interior architect Nathalie Van Reeth, created a destination that pays attention to light, colour, natural materials and texture.

The winding route towards the lodge is majestic, meandering through the mountains of the Cairngorms National Park and past whisky distilleries and across Gairnshiel Bridge, a steep arched bridge built five years after the lodge was completed in the mid-18th century. It feels like not much has changed since then.

Not content on simply making a beautiful interior, it was indeed a feeling that the owners wanted to imbue in the new space. They were inspired by renowned Belgian designer Axel Vervoordt, who believes a tenet of designing a home is that the owner feels at one with it, that it is a part of themselves.

The owners' son Maarten spent two years studying interior architecture and working under Vervoordt, a master at rediscovering the forgotten and giving it a better place.

Here, the traditional sits in harmony with the modern and the interior blends seamlessly into the rugged atmosphere of nature and the River Gairn, which thunders breathlessly by its front door. Primitive antiques sit beside designer pieces, while monochromatic colour schemes create calm spaces that come alive with rustic textures and the play of natural light through the day. The gentle touch of metallic lighting illuminates spaces with a subtle yet captivating energy by nightfall, whispering stories of elegance and modernity.

A Belgian sensibility and Eastern philosophies have informed the space, including the concept of wabi-sabi, from the values of Zen monks in Japan, who sought contentment in simplicity, purity and restraint – a celebration of beauty in humble things. Primitive antiques sit beside designer pieces.

In the lounge, a Belgian linen-covered sofa is surrounded by vintage designs, including a Kristian Vedel black leather and rosewood Modus chair. The walls here and throughout are finished with Crustal, a chalk-based 'mineral coating' that feels otherworldly and creates a perfect foil for the beautiful artefacts and antiquities that rest in front of it.

The dining room's four-metre table was designed by Van Reeth and custom-made in Antwerp. It's surrounded by vintage chairs and Pierre Chapo stools. The stone walls are all original, while in the bathroom, the surfaces – walls, floors, counters, bathtub surrounds – are finished with a stucco-like, water-resistant material.

The meditation here was to create warm but pure spaces. Proving that nature is, in fact, the greatest master, Gairnshiel manages to capture the spirit of its surroundings.

Stone and wood set the tone in the former Victorian hunting lodge boot room.

*The old world inspires me to create
a new world.*
Axel Vervoordt

*Above left: the austere
and textural limewash
walls allow the rooms to
breathe. Above right: the
bar is finished in hand
woven raffia with vintage
wicker stools.*

A Belgian linen sofa sits
alongside black leather and
rosewood chairs. The walls
are finished with a chalk-
based mineral coating.

Pityoulish House

THE CAIRNGORMS

———

Earth House

Pityoulish House, a name derived from ancient Pictish that is said to mean 'bright, beautiful gathering place,' is the story of a home and its owners returning its roots. Salem Avan was born in the Gorbals in Glasgow in the late 1960s and left Scotland three decades ago, ending up in a number of war zones working with the UN. Along with his partner Dianne, he yearned for a sense of home and decided to swap sunny California for the Cairngorms.

The Picts, early medieval people, lived in Scotland in the Iron Age for around 600 years from 300 CE. The grounds surrounding Pityoulish are abound with archaeological remains and its new owners eel the same spiritual reverence the civilisation may have felt then, suggested by the sacred sites dotted around here.

The River Spey is perhaps most known for its salmon fishing and whisky production but Pityoulish commands its best view, high above its most dramatic bend. The home is hugged on two sides. 'The energy of the river has passed by and through this site for millennia – the trees are ancient and feel very much like they contribute to the feeling of the place.'

At 300 years old, the home is comparatively younger than its ancient site, but its history adds to its mystery and it's what drew these homeowners in. Despite being divided into separate tribes, the Picts were said to be a relatively peaceful people, with battles most likely to occur over minor incidents like livestock raiding.

What happened between 300 CE and today remains somewhat of a mystery. When Salem and Dianne first saw the house it had been neglected for several decades and, with rain pouring in through a damaged roof, it was in a state of accelerating decay.

'We saw it on a dark rainy Scottish night and to say it plainly, the house was scary.' Salem explains, 'After we had walked through the house, I went inside, by myself, to its darkest part to see if I was okay with it and Dianne, was outside. She thought the house was awful and beyond hope and at that moment, a huge stag appeared from behind the house, stood and stared right at her. It was an almost unbelievable moment and we have never seen a stag there since. At that moment I walked out of the house and said, "It's perfect".'

When we originally bought the house there were a lot of difficult and complex energies in there, and slowly we have managed to change the energy to one that is overwhelmingly about love.

The apothecary sitting area with Tibetan singing bowls looks out into the grounds through black Crittall windows.

Soon enough there were rocks, sticks, leaves, shells and other found objects all over the house and that's how we like it. We cycle them out periodically but ultimately, we feel there is nothing we can create that is more beautiful than what is in nature. The process of creating the space was massively rewarding.

A pared-back kitchen and sitting area is enriched with reclaimed stadium flooring from Edinburgh.

Much of the house has been changed. They kept the main walls, replaced the roof and inside, all the plaster and lath had to be removed, even the dooks (wooden plugs) had to come out since they were wet through. It took the house almost a year to dry out.

Salem and Dianne reconfigured all the rooms. Originally the house had around ten bedrooms and four bathrooms, now the house has eight en suite rooms and two cloakrooms. Replacing all the plumbing, electricity, heating and water supply and modernising it to current standards was a big job. All the walls were lime plastered and thankfully they were able to retain the pitched pine floor with supplementary reclaimed flooring coming from a church and Meadowbank stadium in Edinburgh.

Salem wanted to go to art college after school but that was not possible, so this house became his degree. Together they decided that the views from every window were incredible and that having a simple pared-down design that was uncluttered and in balance was the way to go, incorporating natural, soft colours with lots of texture, so the outside was in harmony with the inside.

The owners undoubtedly feel the magic of this home and are often spellbound by the patterns the light makes throughout. Their granddaughter, however, is convinced actual magic is taking part here, with Dianne's potions in the apothecary. Once the rod room, where fishermen would bring their catch, keep their rods and supplies, Dianne decided it would be an apothecary and has slowly collected herbs and plants that grow on the property, making them into medicinal and floral remedies. She creates room sprays for when the children visit and has a copper still from Portugal that is used for distillation of essential oils and essences.

The apothecary has a number of large Crittall windows and for newfound designer Salem it felt right to create a place that has rich dark colours on the walls and natural materials around the fireplace.

For Salem and Dianne, most houses they have lived in are just that: houses. To them, this house is more. 'It felt from the beginning like we had to befriend it, that we had to create trust and bring back love. The house still has her moments – some days she is kind and warm and friendly, other days it feels like the energy is a little more complex and dynamic and we just wait until she calms down again. The house was made with love, for love and as crazy as it might sound, we feel that the house knows that.'

Far left: the curved shower room sits in the centre of the home. Right: woven hanging chairs look out towards the field beyond.

Q&A with Dianne Dain and Salem Avan

————

Favourite spot to enjoy what you've created?

The kitchen is the place where everyone hangs out; we light a fire and let the kids run around and the babies crawl while everyone talks and laughs.

Dream Scottish house guest?

Ewan McGregor, because we share a love of motorcycles and have been to some mad places – it would be fun to share stories.

Who is spinning on the record player?

Every morning Dianne plays the gong and her harp as well as Tibetan bowls, but as far as music that is playing, if we had to choose, it would be Led Zeppelin and Johnny Cash. We are not strictly a Cash only establishment, but almost.

House drink?

We have friends who have the North Point Distillery, so we love everything that they make.

Somewhere close to play?

Our house, but if we had to choose another, there is a magical place on the banks of Loch Ness called Inverfarigaig.

Somewhere in Scotland to stray?

We love to walk up towards Ben Macdui and the Cairngorms and we also love going to the Barn at Rothiemurchus, which feels like home.

Raeburn House

EDINBURGH

———

Viva la Stockbridge

Stockbridge was once a village beyond the medieval Old Town in Edinburgh, surrounded by farmland and home to a small tanning industry and a flour mill. Now it is bounded by New Town, as its cobbled streets and charming Georgian stone terrace rows began drawing the bohemian set. One of those artists was Sir Henry Raeburn, who served as the portrait painter of King George IV of Scotland. To feed his obsession with architecture and gardening he set about developing property in a neoclassical style, and he is responsible for creating the elegant crescent that Lisa Guest and her husband call home.

Lisa has finally found a home in this lofty terrace house, attributing its style to her travels, combining classic European heritage with mid-century modern pieces like those she grew up with at home in Nevada. An eclectic mix of gilded, gold-framed portraits and landscapes on oil hangs on the walls, and while mixing classic patterns and oversized art adds to the historical charm, deeper muddy colours give it a contemporary feel.

Stockbridge is a long way from Las Vegas, where Lisa was born. It was a whirlwind romance for the couple, who met at a Hogmanay party and were married seven months later, with a baby arriving soon after. The romance led them on a property hunt through Edinburgh and it was love at first sight for this leafy street and its established ash trees. The front door, framed by Grecian columns, might be reminiscent of Caesar's Palace on the strip, but all comparisons end there. Lisa and her husband have preserved many of the original details of the home while adding their own eclectic touch.

The couple bought the house from an architect who had lived there for 56 years. He kept the floor plan intact and most period features were in good condition. It took two and a half years for them to put their own stamp on the property. Before they could get to the fun part, they had to add a new roof and an

unexpected addition to their list, replacing the cupola (rounded glass dome). The woodwork inside was dried and decaying, so the doors and architraves were extensively restored and kept unpainted, retaining a warm, timber finish.

When it comes to decorating, Lisa says, 'I like to think how I want the space to make me feel and work backwards from there'. Warm, romantic and sophisticated, but most of all comforting, this home has been layered with history and unexpected modern designer touches. A tight colour palette has been employed here, with dirty greens and warm neutrals making the backdrop to the natural textures of jute, linen and bouclé working alongside sumptuous velvet and rich wood tones. The design style is traditional but eclectic and there is a creative tension here, a play between masculine and feminine, modern and classic, old and new.

Stone and wood are the main ingredients in the kitchen here, peppered with plants and pottery. The La Cornue range is its beating heart, but it's the warm and worn wooden table that steals the show and is the scene of many of this home's most memorable moments. The stone floor, honed tiles and white cabinets all help to make this space feel relaxed.

Lisa has drawn on her deep love of nature to create a home that feels quiet and calm. She abides by the tenets of slow living and has created a happy, healthy home that prioritises space, materials and light to create balance. Statement overhead lighting makes an impact, but it's the abundance of lamps and candles that help to create the atmospheric mood.

The farmyards and flour mills of Stockbridge past have long gone, but its creative spirit pulses from this home and onto the leafy, cobbled streets. Cheesemongers and coffee shops sit alongside vintage lamp emporiums and farmer's markets and provide an endless stream of inspiration. For Lisa, the neighbourhood is her muse.

A vintage tub chair has been reupholstered in rich velvet fabric to create the homeowner's favourite spot.

Moody and muddy paint and paper is punctuated with gold and wooden accents.

The handsome facade looks out onto ash trees while the outdoors are brought inside with vintage autumnal fabrics.

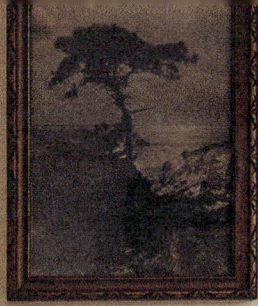

Q&A with Lisa Guest

———

Favourite spot to enjoy what you've created?

The mohair chair in the kitchen where I have my morning coffee and the sitting room – or is it the drawing room? – looking out of the three windows in the summer when the trees are in bloom.

Who is spinning on the record player?

The Smiths or Brandi Carlile, with a sprinkling of Warren G.

House drink?

Spicy margarita.

Dream Scottish house guest?

This is going to sound so cheesy but I honestly enjoy my husband's company the most. I love hearing what he has to say, I find him endlessly interesting.

Somewhere close to play?

Radicibus does really delicious homemade Italian food. Giovanni and his wife run it and they are just lovely. It's super-small and intimate, with the best service.

Somewhere in Scotland to stray?

The Highlands have my heart. The wild, rugged, untouched landscape is so pure and feels healing. Having moved from the desert I'm still amazed nothing is irrigated. I try and get up there by myself for a few days each year to clear the head and recharge.

Boath House

AULDEARN, NAIRNSHIRE

———

Escape Artist

Claude Monet has Giverny, Frida Kahlo has La Casa Azul and Jonny Gent has Boath House. An abandoned hotel, a place to vanish and a refuge for creatives were all on the moodboard for this Highland hideaway. Conceived by swashbuckling artist Gent, this 19th-century manor near the Victorian seaside town of Nairn on Scotland's north coast is a hotel, artists' retreat and blank canvas – an antidote to the archetypal Highland lodge.

The Georgian mansion, originally built for a baronet, was a private house until the 1990s when it was turned into a purple, tartan-clad hotel. Along came Jonny Gent who created this pared-back space, restoring the original features, including its arched windows and dome-vaulted ceiling, and returning the building to a neutral palette. Brown furniture, natural jute and relaxed curtains form the backdrop to its ever-changing art collection. The only condition of a residency here is that you leave something behind. Guests are even left paper and pencils with which to create their own masterpiece and something suggests it's the kind of place you could scribble on a wall and be celebrated, not scolded.

Gent describes the hotel as a 'bolt hole in the woods for the lost artist to start again'. Pinned on the wall are works created by his mates and visitors alike, from Gary Ward to Julian Schnabel. There's not a television in sight, and the analogue hotel also asks its guests to leave the world behind when they walk through the door. It's a far cry from Gent's Sessions Art Club in London, and even further from the Slow and Easy, the Cheshire pub where he grew up.

Painting, pottering in the orchard, wild swimming, rowing, badminton, art, food, music and pleasure are the main ingredients here. The real aim for Gent was to create a portal to the imagination and his method was simple: Remove everything; read more; paint more; play more music, and never look at Pinterest.

The Georgian facade, originally built for a baronet, stands handsomely in established gardens.

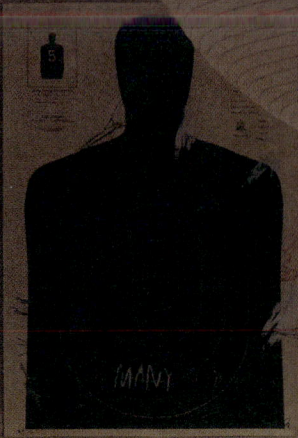

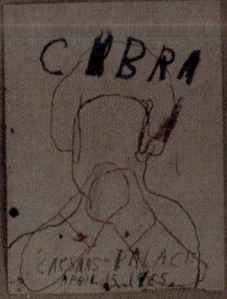

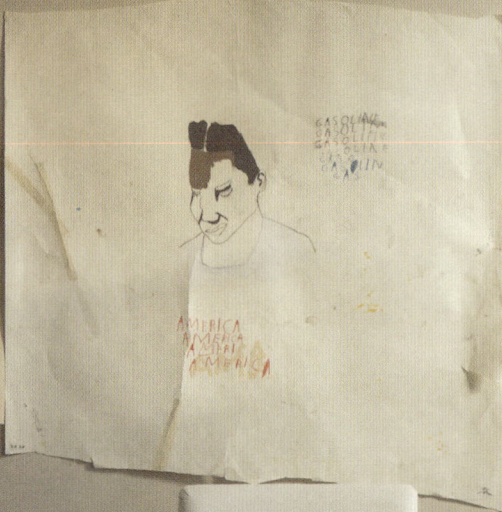

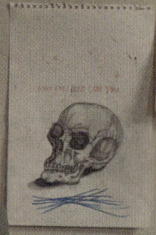

Left: artists are invited to make their mark on the space and leave work behind. Right: a motley crew of velvet toad chairs gather underneath a Ginger Baker lamp, a tribute to the 1960's drummer from Cream.

Above: un-precious vignettes and furniture dot the space. Right: bright white walls invite light to cast their artful rays across the spaces.

Q&A with Jonny Gent

————

Design muse?

Joan of Arc, the smell of oil paint, Townes Van Zandt lyrics, the river and the way cowboys and cowgirls walk.

Favourite spot to enjoy what you've created?

A secret wood on Dalcross estate – a great place to snooze and drown in chanterelles.

Who is spinning on the record player?

Today:
Billie Marten, 'Devil Swim'
Adrianne Lenker, 'Sadness as a Gift'
Juni Habel, 'Drifting Pounds of the Train'
Daughter, 'Dandelion'
Flyte, 'Speech Bubble'
Monks of the Abbey of Notre Dame, Introit Benedicta Sit
Sun Kil Moon, 'Dogs'
Helado Negro, 'I Just Want to Wake up With You'

Dream Scottish house guest?

Alan, our head gardener.

House drink?

Our own birch sap cordial with two shots of vodka, on ice.

Somewhere close to play?

Auldearn Antiques – an old church full of beautiful things.

Somewhere in Scotland to stray?

Pine pools on the river Nairn – fish for salmon, and swim in the deep pools at sunset.

The Lengths

ACHAPHUBUIL, LOCHABER

———

Art School

The Lengths is a modernist building on the shore of Loch Eil. Once a primary school, it serves as home, work studios, creative space and self-catering accommodation for Susie Brown and Ziggy Campbell. Something is always being created here, whether sound installations, films, albums, visual art or furniture. In the past they have had ceramicists, painters, composers, writers, photographers and sculptors staying here and making work.

Previously the couple stayed in rented accommodation in Edinburgh, living month to month while keeping their eyes peeled for unusual buildings to buy in the hope they could get out of the rental loop. When they came across this building their landlord had just given them notice that he was moving back in, so their fate was sealed and they took the leap.

Between them, the couple have undertaken every role of the project from the heavy building work and plumbing to the burning of each individual exterior cladding board and designing and building the kitchen and furniture.

Sticking to the principles of the modernist movement, they kept to a minimal palette and looked at the building inside and out as one work of art. They designed the space to be functional without unnecessary ornamentation, using materials honestly and making sure those materials were relevant to the landscape the building sits within.

Wood, stone, concrete and brick are the chosen materials, and wherever the couple introduced new elements to the building they used reclaimed materials that are sympathetic to its era and style, for example the reclaimed York stone crazy paving in the rear courtyard and brick planters and pond. The build was long, with a particularly intense period for the first five years.

They wanted people to feel really connected to the landscape in the large project space, which is glazed on both sides with views into the ancient woodlands at the back and views over the loch at the front. The kitchen, snug and bedroom areas are more 'hide' like, letting you hunker down.

Susie and Ziggy have created a bunch of smaller, more intimate areas to hang out in while using the large former classroom space as a multifunctional project space to create in. They have been there for 10 years and are still working on areas, although more intermittently. 'We could only have achieved what we have with the incredible help we received from family and friends. We've had many excellent DIY parties along the way.'

We were strict about retaining the original modernist look and feel of the space. Even in its abandoned state the building had a certain charisma, and we wanted to stay true to that.

A 1950's Percival Lafer armchair catching the rays.

We both come from a fine art background
and approached the renovation like we would
any other creative project, experimenting
with materials and giving it all we had. It was
an adventure. I think living in the space right
from the get-go gave us more of a realistic
idea of how we would use each area.

*Above left: a modern
science lab with pegboard
acts as a kitchenette.
Above right: honeycomb
tiles with timber and brass
fittings create a warm and
compact bathroom. Right:
a music studio with vintage
tapestry is topped off with
the original grid ceiling
and opaline lights.*

*We have retained original features where we
felt it worked, from the bifolding doors and
metal split-level divider to the cloakroom
school benches. There were elements of the
modular building structure that were visible,
which we have made more of a feature of.
I think this is one of the most successful
design decisions we landed on.*

Q&A with Susie Brown and Ziggy Campbell

———

Favourite elements you brought to the space?

The vintage German light switches – I was delighted when I found these switches. They came from an old German factory and from the Bauhaus era. The mid-century tapestry in the bedroom – just before we left Edinburgh I came across a pop-up shop where a collector was trying to downsize his hoard and this was hiding in a corner. We had to sleep under it for six months while we stayed with a friend waiting for the sale of the building to go through. Totally worth it. And the poured concrete floor – we poured the 260m² floor with the help of four of our good friends. We had three industrial-sized paddle mixers and 45 minutes per pour before it went off. Then we all stayed over in the only available corner of the empty building while it set properly. What a feat. It's full of good memories.

Design muse?

Scottish designers James Morris, Robert Steedman and Peter Wormsley.

Favourite spot to enjoy what you've created?

The front porch provides great cover to watch a storm over the loch. During longer days in the summer months the window frames cast strong, angular shadows across the large project space and make the whole building seem like an architectural drawing.

Who is spinning on the record player?

Erland Cooper, AVAWAVES, John Carpenter, Vince Guaraldi, Vince Clark and Kathryn Joseph.

Dream Scottish house guest?
Alasdair Gray.

House drink?

A good strong negroni.

Somewhere close to play?

Ardgour Ales makes the best pizza and brews some very tasty beer. On a summer's evening you can sit under the canvas, eat, drink and watch the sunset over the loch.

Somewhere in Scotland to stray?

The places we love the most are the hidden glens and rivers running over giant rocks – and we can't give up their locations.

Gleneagles

AUCHTERARDER, PERTHSHIRE

———

Roaring Twenties

Gleneagles was dubbed the Riviera of the Highlands when it first opened in 1924. The hotel has played host to film directors, diplomats and London's high society who have decamped here over the decades for a spot of golf. From a Christian Dior fashion show in the 1950s to The Gleneagles Agreement in 1970, where the Commonwealth nations met to campaign against apartheid in South Africa, it has fitted a great deal into its 100-year history.

Commissioned by the Caledonian Railway Company, whose General Manager Donald Matheson imagined a grand country house complete with a golf course after falling in love with the area while on holiday. The palatial playground, as it was in the 1920s, is still dedicated to the pursuit of pleasure and leisure. After a long day on the golf course or walking the surrounding Ochil Hills, guests can kick off their muddy stilettos and don their finest glad rags to immerse themselves in good old-fashioned modern glamour. The interiors are certainly not trapped in the past, and the hotel has been brought roaring into the 2020s.

The handsome Gatsby-inspired American Bar is the former luggage store. Excess baggage is no longer welcome here; instead you'll find jazz and cognac. The salon exudes luxury, with heavy curtains, cashmere-clad walls, deep armchairs and a black, foxed mirror and marble bar slinging imaginative cocktails. The menu is even inspired by the pocket encyclopaedias and Observer guides of the era.

A favourite spot for design director Charlie North is the Strathearn with its changing mood throughout the day.

In the morning, I love having my breakfast in the Orangery as the morning light is unbeatable. In the evening, the Strathearn transforms into a sophisticated and elegant world. I always feel like I've stepped back in time when sitting down for dinner with the finest examples of Scottish cuisine and the most exceptional service I've experienced – it's honestly magical. Charlie North

The light-filled orangery bursts to life in trailing flower motifs, soft fabrics and honed marble checkerboard floor.

It's a far cry from 1930s and 40s when World War II forced the hotel to close and become a military hospital, and later a rehabilitation centre for miners. It eventually reopened under strict Ministry of Food rationing orders.

Today, the interiors are rich, layered and well curated, helping it to feel like your country house pile. The pink powder rooms are like stepping into Vivien Leigh's dressing room, upholstered in decadent pleated fabric with floral carpet, chequerboard marble and adorned in tassels, helping it to earn the title of Scotland's most flamboyant loo. The hotel is also fittingly fancy enough for a family of fictional billionaires, playing host to HBO's *Succession* on their Scottish sojourn.

With its opening gala ball broadcast on BBC Radio and hailed the 'the eighth wonder of the world', it feels like the house party is only just beginning.

The American Bar is drenched in dark colours, rich leather and moody mirrors, inspired by 1920's Art Deco glamour.

Sumptuous furnishings in grand, lofty spaces hark back to the golden years, with a decidedly modern update with colours and foliage inspired by the local countryside.

Q&A with Charlie North, design director

Design muse?

It's not a place or a person but a thing. I always take my film camera with me on every trip and it works well to slow me down and notice the smaller details. It's helped to hone my eye, and I have some great travel memories as a result.

Who is spinning on the record player?

A grand piano tinkles in the background, a soft serenade which completes the atmosphere. I also love hearing the occasional 'happy birthday' on the piano – I'm always so proud that people choose to celebrate special occasions there.

Dream Scottish house guest?

Ewan McGregor because I love his motorcycle travel diaries – he always inspires road trips, which I love. For someone a little more historic, I would love to quiz Alexander Graham Bell. We pay tribute to him, and other inventors, at Ochil House, one of the event spaces we designed at Gleneagles.

House drink?

Macallan 18 years old on the rocks, because we're in Scotland. Scotch and soda if we're in for a long night.

Somewhere close to play?

I love an afternoon at the Gleneagles Shooting Lodge for a spot of lunch on the barbecue and clay pigeon shooting with friends, in all seasons.

Somewhere in Scotland to stray?

A drive up to Glencoe for incredible views. I've been lucky enough to drive through Glencoe a few times and it's so special. Pitching a tent on the roof of a Land Rover Defender was a truly magical experience, and waking up to a view of the mountains is breathtaking.

Fife Arms

BRAEMAR, ROYAL DEESIDE

———

Wild Imaginarium

The former Victorian coaching inn has been imaginatively restored inside and faithfully resuscitated outside.

Robert Louis Stevenson first put pen to paper on his novel *Treasure Island* in the bucolic village of Braemar, now more famous for the Fife Arms, a flamboyant, full-fat Scottish hotel with a twist of Picasso. The world's finest contemporary art sits beside Scottish heritage crafts in this Victoriana wonderland. That's what happens when Iwan and Manuela Wirth, of internationally acclaimed art gallery Hauser & Wirth, buy the only coaching inn in the village.

First opened in 1856, The Fife Arms became popular as Queen Victoria began her excursions to nearby Balmoral there after Prince Albert bought her the estate and castle. Later falling out of favour, it was a local pub and rest stop for weary bus tourists until, swapping pilgrims for Porsches, today's hotel emerged to become the design destination for art aficionados with an adventurous streak. Perched beside the River Dee, renowned for its salmon fly fishing, the Fife Arms is nuzzled by the ancient Grampian Mountains in the magnificent Cairngorms National Park.

The interiors are at once outlandish and fantastical, devised by the imaginarium of Russel Sage and Hauser & Wirth. A flying stag with swan wings leaps from the bar, while each room pays homage to a great Scot, from Stevenson to heroine Flora Macdonald, who helped Bonnie Prince Charlie over the sea to Skye.

Art plays an important part here. Enter the drawing room to be met with tartan-clad walls, only to glance up and find a technicolour ceiling mural inspired by agates of ancient Scottish quartz from Chinese artist Zhang Enli. Watercolours from Queen Victoria hang beside Pablo Picassos, while Freud and Richter look on.

Despite art and influences from around the world, you could only be in the Scottish Highlands here, caber tossing at the Braemar Gathering Highland Games or birding and hiking the surrounding mountains and, at night, sipping a dram and bruising the floorboards with a ceilidh.

The building itself was rescued from its unsympathetic 20th-century coaching inn days over four years by Moxon Architects, who carefully restored its granite fabric while resuscitating its Arts and Crafts details, creating a stage set for its imaginative second act. Russell Sage reclaimed the original floors and fireplaces but much of the inside has been reimagined, guided by historians. Where fireplaces have been added, they have been turbocharged with Scottish history, such as a monumental chimney piece from Leven in Fife depicting the life of Rabbie Burns.

Culture, art and history are mashed together here in the most wonderful way. There are 16,000 delightfully eccentric antiques, art pieces and curios, from a pipe carved by Burns to a vanity set from Italian fashion designer Elsa Schiaparelli.

An abundance of pattern, a menagerie of sumptuous textiles, deliciously bold wall coverings and a healthy serving of taxidermy (mandatory for a Highland hotel) are thrown together here and somehow it just works, taking you on a flight of fancy through each room. This is modern Victoriana in all its splendour, with a dash of romance and humour for good measure.

William Morris Acanthus
adds to the Arts and Craft
aesthetic while a herd of
taxidermy fills the walls.

The world's finest contemporary art sits beside Scottish heritage crafts in this Victoriana wonderland. That's what happens when Iwan and Manuela Wirth, of internationally acclaimed art gallery Hauser & Wirth, buy the only coaching inn in the village.

———

Ardoch Steading

UPPER DEESIDE, ABERDEENSHIRE

———

Auld & New

Tom Weir, Scottish climber and author, said, 'At the end of a very steep climbing track (Ardoch's) fields command what must be one of the finest views in the Scottish Highlands'. Overlooking the River Dee near Braemar in the Cairngorms National Park, the compact hillside 'fermtoun' (farm settlement) of Ardoch has been restored, reinstated and reinvented for the 21st century.

The main farmhouse was built by the Duguid family in the mid-1850s, succeeding an ancient single room 'blackhouse' built into the hillside behind. The track leading up to and beyond the farm was laid for Queen Victoria, in order that she could look down on Balmoral from the top of Creag a' Chlamhain.

In the latter half of the 20th century Ardoch was home to Jean Bain and her son Rob Bain. Mrs Bain was the last speaker of Deeside Gaelic, a distinct highland dialect thought to be extinct several decades earlier, while Rob farmed the surrounding hills his whole life. The buildings later fell into disrepair, becoming a danger to anyone who ventured through the site to the top of the hill above.

The buildings and site have been restored following a decade-long project of reconstruction and replanting. Artist Naomi Mcintosh and architect Ben Addy of Moxon Architects, alongside a team of talented craftspeople, used a combination of traditional and contemporary methods to renew or repurpose the buildings within a specifically highland vernacular footprint.

Working from the outside in, the first job was to repair the site – by planting 450 native trees and by protecting 50 rare aspen suckers, a conservation priority species, from grazing by the deer that wander through the site each night. And reinstate the kailyaird – a highland potager garden. Then the buildings: stabilise or reconstruct the walls, rebuild the collapsed roofs. Finally occupy those buildings with meaningful and enjoyable new spaces and uses.

Pre-dating the main house by 20–30 years, the steading is a solid 'L' plan former byre in granite and slate that has been repurposed as an additional study/living space and accommodation for friends and family. The partially collapsed walls and roof have been rebuilt to the original form, while previously blocked-up doorways have been re-opened.

Using only the original apertures in the walls, the steading has been re-purposed while maintaining intact the surviving fabric. Frameless glass preserves the vernacular form of the openings that can now be shuttered during winter storms. The interior has been rebuilt, with the pre-existing volumes as a template for the new living spaces.

The living room and study occupy one double height wing of the L, centred on a new fireplace with frameless glass windows. A ground level bathroom suite and upper level bed loft complete the other wing.

There were three big material deliveries on this project: clay plaster and oak line the entirety of the interior, with the exception of the bathroom where riven caithness slabs are laid to the floor and ceramic to the walls. Oak joinery conceals modern appliances and fittings, prioritising the experience of the space.

Over the last century and a half these buildings have been occupied by tenant farmers, professional gardeners and at one time the Queen's seamstress. Each had a different way of living there, and the same goes for the current and doubtless future inhabitants. So, durability (in all senses) was important to the owners: 'For us this also means flexibility, as the longest lasting buildings have an inherent capacity for being repurposed: times change over the course of a building's lifetime and inhabitant's requirements evolve'.

These are tough and extremely well-built buildings made mostly from materials found on the hillside above. The track for bringing granite down for construction is still just about visible in the woods. Where the masonry has been rebuilt the stone has again come from the site itself – zero material miles. Similarly, wind-blown cherry and ash from the garden has been turned to form door handles and other joinery details.

For Ben and Naomi, most of all, it is about continuity in the 'art of building' embodied by the existing buildings. For what are ostensibly humble vernacular structures the precision of the original construction is remarkable – the 'as built' geometry of the windows, walls and roofs is millimetre perfect, which is unusual for this type of building: 'It was important that the new parts brought forward the same sensibilities'.

Oak joinery conceals much of the inner workings and preserves the minimal, rural aesthetic.

*Clay plaster and a quiet
colour palette create calm
spaces to retreat.*

Q&A with Naomi McIntosh, artist

Three favourite elements you brought to the space?

The Garden: we have old photos of the garden given to us by George Duguid, who was born in the house, showing the original vegetable beds. We have reinstated them and are now gardening in the same way.

Light: for our plants in the garden and greenhouse and for ourselves. The windows are frameless and make use of the full extent of wall openings, interior surfaces are plain to receive shadows and the movement of the sun.

Quiet interventions: the steading plan has remained almost exactly as it once was – just the use of the building has changed. We have not made any new window openings – it is all original – but where there was once a barn door, there is now a piece of glass.

Design muse?

The surrounding landscape is our muse. Living here for over a decade, slowly restoring and rebuilding the ruined outbuildings, replanting the garden – our understanding of this place developed over time and influenced every decision we made. Their position of the outbuildings on a grassy shelf on the hillside, as well as their relationship to each other, was completely in tune with the landscape and climate. The main house sits on the axis of the glen – you look straight down the centre of the valley – and all the other buildings cluster around in a mutually sheltering way, creating wind breaks and kitchen gardens.

Favourite spot to enjoy what you've created?

There's a cherry tree above the site with some conveniently flat granite boulders beneath it – it was where we first sat and looked at the place before we moved here. The view looks over the buildings, garden and across the River Dee to Lochnagar.

What music is playing?

The Deeside fiddle player and composer Paul Anderson. His beautiful compositions speak to the landscape of Deeside and the Cairngorms – his music sounds like home.

Dream Scottish house guest?

The previous inhabitants of this place – the Duguids and the Bains. We feel responsible as temporary caretakers for this place and would be fascinated to spend time with those who have also loved this hillside home.

House drink?

I have a ritual of gathering herbs for teas and infusions. I started simply with mint but now our herb garden is growing and it is a beautiful way to notice the changing of the seasons and dry the herbs to capture summer.

Somewhere close to play?

Tarmachan Café in Crathie. It is magical, nestled in the birch trees, and the welcome and atmosphere is so warm. There is an emphasis on seasonal, local produce as well as excellent coffee. To walk to a supper club on the roof top on a summer evening is so special.

Somewhere in Scotland to stray?

Lochnagar is our favourite mountain. It is our view and my anchor. The cliffs of the corrie are breathtaking. We walk to the top from the front door and have a New Year's Eve tradition of a climb, whatever the weather!

Acknowledgements

————

BANJO BEALE

To Scotland, thank you for giving me the most amazing second chapter. To the people of Mull, who have welcomed me in as one of their own, albeit with confused looks on their faces, thank you for giving me a home.

To the homeowners and spacemakers who have opened their doors and invited us into their world, thank you for having us. Your generosity to hold space with us and share your story has made this book a magical journey. Your commitment to craft, history and design is a huge source of inspiration to me.

To Alex, my collaborator and muse – your ability to create warmth in the coldest of places is awe-inspiring. I love seeing the world through your eyes.

To my editor Sophie Allen, thank you for believing in me, twice. You are the wind beneath my wings. To the mighty talented Gemma Hayden who weaved our words and images into this handsome book, you are a magician.

There are a handful of people who have crossed my path, who really saw something in me, even when I didn't see it myself: Michelle Ogundehin, Donna Clarke, Carline Wallice, Clare Mottershead, Steve Allen, Paul Chappell, Andrew Sidwell – thank you for seeing and believing.

To Chris Reade, who tells me to do it and figure it out later, thank you. I will be forever grateful to you and your family for letting us make a home at Sgriob-ruadh.

Dearest Ro, thank you for believing in me, for keeping me honest and always diving headfirst into our next adventure. To Grampa, thanks for being by my side every step of the way.

To my mum and dad, thank you for telling me to dream and enduring me as I rearranged your house every weekend as a little boy. Yours will always be my home.

ALEXANDER BAXTER

To James, my rock in all things – words are not enough. My ever patient and beautiful mother, Angeline; my talented and sparkling sister, Connie; my steadfast and wonderful grandmother, Marie; and my fantastic family. These people are my crew, and they mean the world to me. Taing mhòr dhuibh uile.

A special thank you to Sophie Allen for believing in me and for all her support, and to Gemma Hayden, the talented designer behind this book. These two have helped us craft a book I could only have dreamed of – I will always be grateful to them.

To Banjo, I could not have asked for a better creative partner on this journey. Your eye, your words, and your good cheer are always a deep joy. You often see the things I miss, and my work is richer for it. I remain so very grateful for our collaboration and all your support – it means such a great deal.

I am so very lucky to have worked with the homeowners and creatives featured in this book, and I heartily appreciate the time and energy they have given me and Banjo as we seek to tell their story. I hope we have done you justice. They show the energy and vitality of Scottish design – they are all stars. Many of these homeowners and designers have worked with me for a number of years. These are relationships I cherish. However, I want to particularly acknowledge the team at WildLand, whose work features heavily in this book. Ruth Kramer, along with the late Thomas Schacht, took a punt on me when I was just getting started. The interiors they introduced me to cementated my love for taking pictures of spaces. I will forever be thankful for the confidence they, and the wider Wildland family, showed in me.

About the Author & Photographer

Banjo Beale is an interior designer, broadcaster and author. He is the winner of BBC's *Interior Design Masters*, judge on *Scotland's Home of the Year,* and author of *Wild Isle Style*. His BAFTA award-winning television series for the BBC, *Designing the Hebrides* has garnered a worldwide audience with a second series on the way. Australian by birth and Scottish by choice, Banjo bases his design practice on the Isle of Mull, working across the UK and beyond.

Alexander Baxter is a photographer and creative director based in Scotland and works internationally. Alexander's work can be found in the pages of *The World of Interiors, The Times, Elle Decoration, Dezeen* and many other magazines. In his private brand and photography practice, Alexander works with a host of leaders in the fields of architecture, design and hospitality.

Thank you to all the spaces featured in the book:

RODEL HOUSE @rodelhouseharris
HMS OWL @hmsowl
WORMISTOUNE @wormistoune
BLUEBELL HOUSE @bluebellgray
LUNDIES HOUSE @lundies.scot
GIFFORD @katiedanger_ @josephdanger
ALLT-A-BHRUAIS @greatglencharcuterie
BARD @bard.scotland
QUINE & LOON COTTAGE @quineandlooncottage
BALLONE CASTLE @anta_architecture @anta_scotland
INVERLONAN @inverlonan
LAMB'S HOUSE @_gras
KYLE HOUSE @_gras @gunnar_gras
KILMARTIN CASTLE @kilmartincastle
OLD DULOCH HOUSE @olddulochhouse @mellischeeseltd
DUN GUAIDHRE @harfordcrossarchitects
FERGUSON @simon_harlow Lee Ivett @_baxendale and
Duncan Blackmore @arrantland @arrantindustries
KINLOCH LODGE @kinloch.scot @kinloch_lodge
GAIRNSHIEL @gairnshiellodge
PITYOULISH HOUSE @earth_house_scotland
RAEBURN HOUSE @interiors.by.lisa.guest
BOATH HOUSE @boathhouse
THE LENGTHS @thelengths_studio @lomond_campbell
GLENEAGLES @thegleneagleshotel
FIFE ARMS @thefifearms
ARDOCH STEADING @moxonarchitects @naomi_mcintosh

Artwork Credits

The publisher has made every effort to credit all the makers, artists and designers whose work appears incidentally in the book and will be more than happy to correct or add any omissions in future reprints.

p.21 Mackerel painting by Christopher Riisager; p.39 Lemon Plate by Liberty; p.41 Stool by Anthropology; Isolation Garden Wallpaper by Bluebellgray; p.42(left) photograph by Stacey Weaver; p.42 (centre) vintage painting bought from Panter and Hall; p.42 (right) Turquoise still life by Lucy Anderson; Lamp (left) by Bluebell Gray; p.45 Sebastian the Lamb and Care Bear; p.47 Artworks by Fi Douglas; p.52 Wall mural by French botanical artist Claire Basler; p.53 Face plate on shelf: Bjorn Wiindblad earthenware wall plaque, Denmark, 1980; P.55 Hans Wegner Papa Bear lounge chair; p.59 David Shrigley, *When Life Gives You A Lemon*, 2021 © David Shrigley. All Rights Reserved, DACS. 2023. Poster available to purchase via www.shrigshop.com; p.59 & 66 Portrait Studio, Martin Parr Foundation, Bristol, 2019 © Martin Parr / Magnum Photos; 101 Copenhagen Sphere Bubl vase; p.61(right) Emer Tumily; 62+66 Good Vibes Neighborhood banner; p.79 + 83 Family Tree by Cat Tams; p.81 Hanging fishing rope sculpture by Mark Cook; Metal leaf lozenge by James Rigler; p.85 Bard Cat Throne; Vintage artworks; p.91 vintage Sanderson wallpaper; Furniture by ANTA; p.123, 124 & 128 Paintings by Kristen Hannesdottir; p.133 Isle Sofa by Studio Ilse; p.133,136 Hans Wegner Papa Bear lounge chair; p.134 & 135 Carl Hansen & Son CH23 dining chair; p.135 Akari Light Sculpture by Isamu Noguchi, model 21A; p141 Artwork of bearded lady; p.143 Mid-century French capiz shell pendant light; 19th century plaster cast, prototype of a Dutch milkmaid bronze bust; Table handmade by local craftsman Simon Bevan from Ardfern; Ceramic candle holders are by Glasgow ceramics artist Claire Henry; 17th century candle holders made from firedogs, re-worked by Darren Ainsworth from Seil Island west Scotland; p.147 Copper bath by William Holland; 19th century painting by unknown artist from Greenland; p.171 Architectural drawing by Sarah Wrigglesworth; Stool by Still Life; p.173 Collage of three fire exit signs by Ty Locke; p.173&175 Stool by Tom Philipson; p.187 Wallpaper by Marthe Armitage; p211 Hans Wegner Papa Bear lounge chair; p214 Morris & Co. The Brook Wallpaper; p.219 – William Morris Artichoke Green Camomile fabric; p.224 and 225 Gary Boath; p.225 Marset Ginger Floor Lamp; p. 221 & 228 Photograph of Dierama pulcherrimum by Kate Friend; p.234 (left) Susan Castillo - made during a residency at the house; 235 Vintage Peruvian Tapestry; p.238 Jean-Baptiste Besançon; p.255 (left) – Watts 1874 Triad wallpaper; p.261(foreground) Carl Hansen & Søn's CH-25 chair by Han's Wegner; p.261 Vipp Pouf; p.261 PK22 Lounge Chair by Fritz Hansen; p.261 & 266 Carl Hansen & Søn's Table Bench, designed by Børge Mogensen; p.263 & 265 CH24 Wishbone dining chairs by Carl Hansen & Søn's, designed by Hans J Wegner.